Joel Prentiss Bishop

Secession and Slavery

Volume II

Joel Prentiss Bishop

Secession and Slavery
Volume II

ISBN/EAN: 9783744731256

Printed in Europe, USA, Canada, Australia, Japan

Cover: Foto ©Suzi / pixelio.de

More available books at **www.hansebooks.com**

SECESSION AND SLAVERY:

OR,

THE EFFECT OF SECESSION ON THE RELATION
OF THE UNITED STATES TO THE SECEDED
STATES AND TO SLAVERY THEREIN;

CONSIDERED AS A

QUESTION OF CONSTITUTIONAL LAW,

CHIEFLY UNDER THE AUTHORITY OF

DECISIONS OF THE SUPREME COURT;

EMBRACING ALSO A REVIEW OF THE PRESIDENT'S PLAN OF RECONSTRUCTION.

BY

JOEL PRENTISS BISHOP,

AUTHOR OF "COMMENTARIES ON THE LAW OF MARRIAGE AND DIVORCE,"
"COMMENTARIES ON THE CRIMINAL LAW," ETC.

BOSTON:
A. WILLIAMS & CO.
1864.

Entered according to Act of Congress, in the year 1864, by
JOEL PRENTISS BISHOP,
in the Clerk's Office of the District Court of the District of Massachusetts.

CAMBRIDGE:
Allen and Farnham, Stereotypers and Printers.

INTRODUCTORY NOTE.

This pamphlet is divided into six chapters, as follows:

Chap. I. *Historical Sketch.*
  II. *The Direct Consequences resulting from the Act of Secession.*
  III. *Some Radical Views considered.*
  IV. *The Effect of Contract between the seceded States returning, and the United States.*
  V. *The Emancipation Proclamation.*
  VI. *Concluding Summary;* also, *Postscript on the President's Plan of Reconstruction.*

As originally written, the pamphlet contained likewise a chapter entitled, "*The Consequences resulting from the War which Secession creates.*" But finding that the insertion of this chapter would make the pamphlet too long, while the chapter itself was too short for an adequate discussion of its subject, I determined to omit it; and, whether it will be hereafter given to the public in an enlarged form or not, the public will learn in due time.

The pamphlet here presented embodies a discussion of the question, which, more than any other, perplexes, at the present moment, the people of this country. Will the people read? Will they reflect? Will they hear a voice which speaks the language of the law, and not the language of the politician? These are questions which will be all answered in the affirmative, before the durable peace we seek, descends to us.

The views which this pamphlet contains, were written out in a somewhat different form before the present civil war had assumed any large proportions. But it was evident that, if published, they would be received with indifference or with scorn by those who should be benefited by them. So the manuscript lay upon my shelves unused. In like manner, this pamphlet, with the exception of the Postscript, has lain by stereotyped for several months, since it was put into this permanent shape in type-metal. Am I still too early? He who rules all things knows; I do not. I sent out, in my "Thoughts for the Times," the first dove; but it returned. Will this one come back? or, if it does, will it bring the olive leaf?

Many readers will object, that this pamphlet is written in a style which lacks gravity, and that it does not so soberly consider serious questions of law as it ought. There are serious legal questions — difficult ones — connected with our present national troubles, but the questions discussed in this pamphlet are of another class. There is, indeed, the serious question, — Shall we obey the law? but there is no difficulty as to what the law is. Politicians may shed darkness upon the matter; but posterity will say, that, among the topics handled in these pages, there is no one which deserved a graver consideration than it has here received. And the great question which this nation is answering, in the presence of earth and of heaven, is, not what the law is, not whether the Constitution which our forefathers made is a wise one, not whether the law of our Constitution ought not to be amended; but it is, *whether the people of this country shall continue to put forth falsehood about a Constitution which they will not either amend or obey.*

J. P. B.

Boston, 1864.

SECESSION AND SLAVERY.

CHAPTER I.

HISTORICAL SKETCH.

The present is a moment at which, if ever during the war, the public mind may be supposed to be prepared to receive some seeds of what the writer of this pamphlet understands to be truth. It is but a few weeks since he put forth another pamphlet, wherein he showed, that, both in war and in peace, it should be our first aim to obey the law of the land. That pamphlet, entitled "Thoughts for the Times," fell on ears which found little time to listen to such an admonition as this. Was not Policy abroad? Why, then, should we care for Law?

Let us look. There are two kinds of law: the first, and that with which the people of this country are happily more familiar than with the other, is the law of peace; the other, is the law of war. The one, is administered in the civil tribunals of the land; the other, is administered in that great hall, redolent with the light of peace, wherein, amid the roar of rolling musketry and choral cannon noise, the souls of the patriot brave wind wreaths of glory on their brows, and many a weary one ascends to his everlasting rest. Over the civil tribunals, Taney, C. J., and some others, at present, preside; over this other tribunal presides, at the present moment, Abraham Lincoln, President of the United States.

When the rebellion, which for a long series of years had been coming silently up, culminated into open acts of treason, the government of the United States was being administered, both in its various civil departments, and in those also which control the war-dealing power, by men of the Democratic party in politics. James Buchanan presided, in theory, over the war-arm; but it was quiescent, and neither he nor anybody else deemed it wise to wake it into action. The civil arm slept with the war-arm; nor did any considerable number of persons, either in power or out of power, think it well to call this arm into motion to punish treason, or arrest the course of the rebellion. This whole nation despised the law, both the law of war and the law of peace; and, led by the Democratic party, and not much remonstrated with by the Republican, caused the administrators of both kinds of law to absent themselves from their respective halls, while the halls were pillaged and blackened by assassins of their country.

There is no harm in sometimes looking back on the past; perhaps a still further view of it may here do us good.

Advocates of free speech and of the utmost freedom of action there were then as now; and these advocates said, — "It is wrong to interfere with men who merely differ from you in politics." So, as the assassins would not check themselves, those who were not assassins — not perceiving the distinction between liberty and license, between walking unrestrained beneath laws which freemen have freely made, and tearing with hands unappointed those laws away — deemed that they must not interfere, the matter being a mere difference in politics!

But while the question of political liberty stood thus, how stood, on the other hand, the question of what may be termed *religious liberty?* Let it be remembered, that, from the beginning of things in this country, we — to wit, a large class of our people — have been zealous and humble followers of a certain old and honored Scripture doctrine, which is best known by the name of the *Curse of Ham.* We have deemed it to be our duty, as heirs of celestial glory, to put forth our terrestrial powers in the divine work of *cursing Ham.* Knowing that God had cursed Ham, we have esteemed it ours to walk in the heavenly footsteps, so we have *cursed Ham. Curse* Ham, *cursing* Ham, *cursed* Ham! By force of these three cardinal points, we became the *Church of the Cursers of Ham.* And as we were diligent workers with the church, and greatly-esteemed members of it, we arose thereby to be *saints.* But as for our saintships there was no rest, the powers of the outer darkness contending continually against us, we became entitled, by the way in which we conducted the combat on our part, to the further appellation of *saints militant*.

Scarcely can the foot of a saint, who is not militant, find repose on the earth. What, then, could be expected where the foot was of one always militant? Why, there came up, in our case, heresies warring against us. A heretic appeared and said, — "Saints should lay up their treasure, not in negroes, but in justice." How could such a heretic be endured? They who, when the present rebellion broke out, were the most clamorous for political freedom, exclaimed, at this earlier time, — "Let the heretic be hung!" Neither had they, when the rebellion had expanded to its full proportions, ceased to cry, "Let the heretic be hung;" while, even at the present moment, they are clamoring in one breath for the hanging of the heretic; and, in the next breath, for more of the same freedom through which treason wrought up rebellion into open war. Always, indeed, from the beginning of this heresy, there have been heretics hung by mobs, shot by mobs, tarred and feathered by mobs, and lied about by the respectable portion of the community; but, when the political heresy of murdering republican liberty arose, there was no man found even to lie about such a heretic. It was a different bull which gored in the one case from that which gored in the other.

There was one instance in which a *heretic militant* — only a few heretics are *militant* — undertook the same course of conduct which was afterward imitated by the saints. This heretic, with a few followers, stole an arsenal. Thereupon all the powers both of Church and State arose! The lion of war shook his shaggy mane! Judicial justice brought out her two cups, and one pivot, and one beam, and put into the downward cup all her weight! Virginia was herself again! In majesty came forth the array of arms! Upon the bench also, in majesty, sat the ministers of the civil power! The heretic militant was laid low! No — he was first swung high on the gallows! It was afterward that he was cut down! And not until he was put away where his palsied fingers could steal no more arsenals, did either the church militant or Virginia give rest to the feet or slumber to the eyes of the ministers of either the war or the civil power! But when, in later stealings of numerous arsenals, " John Brown's soul was seen still to be marching on," how quietly slept these two great powers which erewhile had jointly executed one entire, fanatical, and heretical stealer of one whole arsenal! Ah, the *church militant* is a particular thing — she may steal! The *heretic militant* is another thing — he may not steal! There is a difference between Jeff. Davis and John Brown! Angels and men! behold the difference! Here is wisdom; look and learn!

Now, while we admit that there is a difference between Brown, the heretic militant, and Davis, the saint militant, — a difference which might justify a diversity of treatment in the two cases, — still for this diversity, as actually exhibited in the conduct of the country, we find no warrant in the Constitution of the United States, or in any law properly existing in any State under the Constitution; it is all matter pertaining to the higher law, as found among the mysteries of the Church of the Cursers!

Neither let me for a moment pretend, that the religious heresy, even where it assumes the ordinary form and is not militant, is not immeasurably worse than the political heresy of plunging the country into war for the sake of destroying the Constitution and saving the Church.

No! It is admitted, that even the milder religious heretic is worse (my reader being now a Catholic) than the reviler of the Sacred Presence in the Eucharist; or (he being a Protestant) than the fulminator of the last Bull; or (he being a Jew) than the believer in Jesus of Nazareth; or (he being a Mormon) than the disbeliever in Joseph Smith. All this is fully conceded. Indeed the heretic of whom I am speaking may, at least for the purposes of this argument, be set down as the king of heretics, the same as, in Hiawatha, the sturgeon is set down as the king of fishes. And I will concede also, that God has raised up Jeff. Davis to slay this heretic, the same as Hiawatha slew the sturgeon.

Still there is one point plain: the course adopted by Davis in conjunction with his followers and compeers, in their attack upon the heretic, was in direct antagonism to, in full violation of, the law of the land. Yet up to the time when the saintly power sent forth from cannon militant the earthly missiles which tore down the flag of our country from Fort Sumter, this nation, in dealing with their saintships, walked in the light of texts of Scripture, or of such other higher gleams as angels hand down to us, and not in the light either of our written Constitution, or of any other recognized earthly law. Indeed, there are still among us large numbers of people who cling to the higher gleams, and despise the lower law of our Constitution.

Let us see what some of these higher gleams, by which we walked, were. One of them was expressed thus: "The government of the United States has no power to coerce a sovereign State." The rabble who make noises, but neither look nor think, were led by the more knowing ones to believe, that this expression was taken, letter for letter, out of that wondrous book of which they had heard, but which they did not expect ever to see, called the "Constitution of the United States."

If you followed up one of these deceivers, he told you, that indeed these words were not in the Constitution, and that the purpose of his harangue was merely to point attention to the fact of their not being there. Well, then, it is admitted that the Constitution does not say, in exact terms, "You may coerce a sovereign State." Suppose it does not; neither does it, in terms, say, "You may shot your cannon with grape." But it provides, that the President shall be commander-in-chief of the land and naval forces of the United States; it provides for the raising of such forces, and therewith, and by other means mentioned, for the President's faithfully executing the laws and causing them to be obeyed. If a State refuses to have her legislators and judges sworn to support the Constitution of the United States,— for so the Constitution directs they shall be sworn,— and if no other available means present themselves, cannot the war-power coerce the State into doing what this "supreme law of the land" declares the State shall do? The Constitution tells the President what shall be his duty, namely, to "take care that the laws be faithfully executed;" it puts into his hands the instrument, namely, the whole war-power of the country, with which to do the duty,— "but, no!" says the deceiver, "he has no right to coerce a sovereign State!" The sovereign State refuses to obey the laws, the President is given the army and navy, and told he must make the State obey; he has sworn that he will faithfully perform what is thus enjoined,— "but, no!" screams again the deceiver, "the words, 'he may coerce a sovereign State,' are not in the instrument;" that is, the country is full of fools who will believe such stuff when knaves tell it to them!

Knaves! I should have said *saints*. A saint knows — who but a saint does? — that it is expressly written in the Constitution, "Thou mayst coerce a son of Ham; and, if any man reviles a Curser of Ham, let him be *crushed out*." Here, if the Constitution is read aright, it establishes an exact form of religion, which religion consists in *cursing Ham*. Therefore, — so the argument runs,— if a "sovereign State," deeming that this cursing of Ham can be best carried on by tearing the nation in two, the United States has no authority to interfere by coercion to arrest such conduct, since the interference would be an act in conflict with the provision establishing the church. So we come to the question, whether, in truth, the provision whereby the church of the cursers is set supreme over all other things, is really in the lower Constitution of the land, or whether it is only in the higher Constitution of the saints.

Let us look at another of these gleamy upper lights, in whose effulgence we walked. It is this: "The chief-justice of the United States is the commander-in-chief of its armies." Now, though this gleam, as I have said, and repeat, springs from the higher fires, not being found in the Constitution of the United States, demagogues have told to gaping crowds, ever since this war began, that it is taken, stroke by stroke, coruscation by coruscation, — taken in mystic letter, — in body, soul, all, — out of the Constitution. These demagogues have told, that Taney, C. J., is entitled to command our national military forces; and that, as often as Abraham Lincoln declines to submit his army orders to Taney's revision and countermand, the Constitution is broken, trampled upon, and all the other evil things which a demagogue can name! But here is a matter involving many considerations of grave import, and I cannot spare space to unfold it further now; therefore, I pass on with the single remark, that Taney, C. J., has not claimed for himself such power; though, in the *Merryman case*, 24 Law Reporter, 78, — a case not well put on the part of the military authorities, — there fell from him some observations somewhat calculated to give the appearance of consent to this higher-law doctrine of the saints on the subject. Whether he will ever regret, or has regretted, that his words were not more guarded, I have no means of knowing; but, be this as it may, there is, in the case, as properly understood, no sufficient warrant for the much-advocated claim of right to cast the civil power across the track of the war-power, and thereby arrest it in its course. The single fact, — which I have not room here to discuss, — that the case was not put before the judge on its true ground, by the military authorities, alone leaves the decision of no weight when applied to cases put on other and correct ground.

When the rebellion first broke out into war, we had it laid down to us, — here is another of the higher gleams, — that the war, on the part of the United States, must be waged as follows: "The army of the Union," said the gleam, "may march to the field of conflict; there, halt; then it must get the names of the several rebels constituting the opposing army; next, cause each one to be indicted by a grand jury of his peers; finally, have each tried before a petit jury, — no, *finally*, after this, — shoot? no — stand by and see the marshal hang the traitors!" Such, we were assured, was the provision of the Constitution! Let us look: Art. V. of the Amendments — this is admitted — reads, "No person shall . . . . be deprived of life, liberty, or property without due process of law;" which words "due process of law" mean — this is likewise admitted — indictment, &c., as just explained. There are other clauses of the instrument which signify also substantially the same thing. Now, was this rule of procedure laid down, in the Constitution, for the guidance of the war power, or of the civil? "For the guidance of both," shouts the demagogue; and a chorus of fools' voices responds "*hurrah!*"

The last expression which I have seen of this demagogical proposition is contained in the protest of Vallandigham against being tried by Gen. Burnside's court-martial. Let me copy it. I find it in the recently published authentic report of the trial. It is as follows:

"Arrested without due 'process of law,' without warrant from any judicial officer [so is every rebel prisoner captured], and now in military prison [so are all the rebel prisoners, except when out on parole]. I have been served with a 'charge and specifications' [so is every rebel spy or other rebel prisoner who is tried after being captured], as in a Court-martial or Military Commission. I am not [nor is Jeff. Davis] in either 'the land or naval forces of the United States, nor in the militia in the actual service of the United States;' and therefore [the old argument against the government's right to interfere, by military power, for the suppression of the rebellion] am not triable for any cause, by any such Court, but am subject, by the express terms of the Constitution, to arrest only by due process of law, judicial warrant, regularly issued upon affidavit, and by some officer or court of competent jurisdiction for the trial of citizens, and am now entitled to be tried on an indictment or presentment of a grand jury of such court, to speedy and public trial by an impartial jury of the State of Ohio, to be confronted with witnesses against me, to have compulsory process for witnesses in my behalf, the assistance of counsel for my defence, and evidence and argument according to the common laws and ways of judicial courts."

The remainder of the protest is not material to the present point.

Vallandigham, being retained by the military

tribunal for trial, and condemned, notwithstanding the protest, applied to the Circuit Court of the United States for a writ of *habeas corpus* to set him at liberty. The court, on full hearing of counsel, refused to grant the writ.[1]

Now, whether it was a judicious exercise of the war-power to extend the line of its operations so far as Dayton, Ohio; and whether, when this power captured Vallandigham as a prisoner of war, trying him by court-martial as it does spies and some other classes of prisoners of war, instead of holding them for exchange, it placed its fangs on an enemy or on a friend, — this I do not propose to discuss. But, as we have seen, when Vallandigham appeared before the military tribunal, demagogism found its chance to speak; and it pronounced, in almost exact terms, the same speech over again which the saintly gleam had employed at the earlier period, in pointing out the way in which loyal stupidity should meet, on the field of conflict, disloyal saintship. And when Vallandigham went thence with his case before the civil tribunal, lo, the heavenly gleam was still with him;

---

[1] See the full Trial, as recently published in Cincinnati. I cannot but recommend it to the perusal of gentlemen who are engaged in inquiries concerning the law of this subject. The argument of Mr. Perry, who appeared as counsel for Gen. Burnside on the application for the *habeas corpus*, is particularly instructive; though I do not mean to say how far I concur in his views. Ex-Senator Pugh, who represented Vallandigham, presented fully the cause of his client; but his argument is subject, at least, to this one observation, that principal points in it had been already, probably unknown to him, decided adversely to his positions by the Supreme Court of the United States. It contains, however, the substance of what could with decency be said on that side of the question, before a judicial tribunal.

and thus spake the gleam through its entranced
demagogism, and said: "I come to you, O Judge,
from out the sainted airs above, to say, that, by the
laws of the upper realm, where I dwell, this court is
supreme over Gen. Burnside and his forces; here is
an order made by the general, the court is com-
manded to revoke the order." Yet the civil tribunal,
not finding the law referred to laid down in the
Constitution, did not decide to usurp jurisdiction
over the military power; but the ——— (let the
blank stand there), determined to overrule both the
civil and the military authorities, to revise and correct
the proceedings of both courts alike; and, in order
to preserve tranquillity throughout the loyal country,
and to rebuke the radicalism of setting up the Constitution above the Church, — to show how loved are
the political doctrines which Vallandigham has been
putting forth ever since this rebellion broke out,
and how much worthier he is esteemed to be than
are all his peers, — to testify likewise to how much
more he knows than do the generals and the judges,
and how much purer of heart he is than they, — to
put him, moreover, if possible, in command of generals and above judges, — finally, to check the
course of this "unholy war," which is leading men
into forgetfulness of the Church, and into too much
regard for the law and the Constitution of the country, — nominated him candidate for governor of
Ohio!

So we get back to the place whence we started.
At the opening of the rebellion, the larger part of
the people said, "Away with both the civil and the

military powers! These rebels are saints-militant; it would be a violation of the higher law, which is above the Constitution of the United States, to interfere with their saintly course; let both the military power and the civil sleep. By and by, the military power was awakened by the cannon which shot away the flag of the Union from Fort Sumter. Then the people who loved the saints, not to say the saints themselves, appealed from the military power, as represented by Lincoln, to the civil power, as represented by Taney. Taney was understood to take sides against Lincoln. From that day downward went up a scream in favor of the civil power. Here, a way was supposed to be found in which the hands of the government could be palsied, and the rebellion and church left to triumph, while the nation was destroyed. "The civil jurisdiction," said the scream, "must be preserved just the same in war as in peace; the courts must be always active, *commanding armies as they do constables and sheriffs;* or our liberties are gone forever!" At length, in the case of Vallandigham, and some other cases, the civil power refused to rush into the fight against the military; so now, as both the civil arm and the war-arm are lost to the Church, the scream explodes thus: "*Let both arms lie palsied in the dust,* or the saint will not succeed in slaying the heretic?"

I hope I shall not be understood, in these observations, as casting reproach upon those conscientious men who, instead of reading the Constitution for themselves, blindly follow unscrupulous leaders; and so believe, what they are told, that the Constitution says, — "The United States shall not coerce a State," — "The judges, and not the President, shall command the army and navy," — "The army may indict, and the like, but must not shoot," — together with the rest of the stuff wherewith demagogues, who want the votes of the saints, undertake to beguile also the sinners.

It is a question of theology, which I do not mean to discuss, whether we may not play false for the glory of the church. Let us admit that we may. Still, if we turn to the Constitution of the United States, we shall search this instrument in vain to find in it the provision authorizing such a procedure in political and governmental matters.

The result to which we come is this: It may be our higher-law, religious duty, as Cursers of Ham, to do one thing, or another thing; but, as citizens of the United States, it is our lower-law duty to look into the Constitution of the United States for ourselves, take no demagogue's word as to what is in it; read it; then obey. In the following chapters, I shall endeavor to give some assistance to such persons, whether lawyers or laymen, as propose to read the Constitution for themselves, in order to understand what is our present relation to the seceded States and to slavery therein. I shall not have occasion to ask my readers to reject any doctrine ever held by any court, or any judge, or any writer on constitutional law; or, indeed, by anybody else, unless we may except some of the demagogues of the present day, whose religious duties, as Cursers of Ham, or whose aspirations after the heaven of office wherewith the church promises to reward her followers, have led them to deny the conclusions to which I would conduct my readers, in such terms as *possibly* to include also some of the premises; though of this exception I am not sure. On the contrary, were I to discuss the subject much more at length than I intend in these pages, I should have only to enforce the doctrines which have already been laid down by the judiciary, by congress, and by writers on constitutional law who have gone before me.

The present pamphlet does not profess to contain a complete juridical discussion of the entire subject. This fuller discussion I reserve for a book, wherein I propose to consider, as a commentator on the law, the several questions of constitutional, and some of the questions of statutory and international law, involved, whether as cause or attendant, in our present civil war. The doctrines of this pamphlet are principally drawn, as its title-page indicates, from the decisions of the highest court known under our Constitution, the Supreme Court of the United States. Though they are put forth in a form semi-popular, they are believed to be as legally exact as if they were dressed in the ordinary garb of a professional treatise. There are questions connected with our present subject, upon which judicial decision has not yet passed. I have avoided the discussion of these questions in order that in this pamphlet nothing might be set down which is not settled law, — settled by the Supreme Court of the United States. Whether there are not parts of our law, — in fact, parts of our Constitution, — the final as well as the immediate interpretation whereof rests with other departments of the government than the judiciary, is a question which I do not propose to discuss in this pamphlet, though it was long since adjudged by the judiciary that there are. In this pamphlet I assume, that, upon all the questions discussed, the Supreme Court of the United States is the ultimate authority.

Had I never seen men before this war broke out; and had I, since the war broke out, been blind and deaf to all which passed before me; I should suppose, that now, since the close of the last sittings of the Supreme Court of the United States, substantial harmony would prevail among all persons who call themselves loyal throughout the country. But, alas! men are not what they profess, things are not what they seem.

There have been among us, from the beginning of this war, men who have clamored against it, as violating the Constitution of the United States; for, they said, that, by the Constitution, there could be no war for the subjugation of rebels in arms in seceded States. Thus, as late as last May, Ex-Senator Pugh, one of the leaders in this class of politics, standing before a judicial tribunal as the advocate of Vallandigham, another leader, in the case mentioned a little way back, put forth the following doctrine, as a full and sufficient answer to whatever could be said, and had been said, against his client: "I affirm, then, distinctly, that the government of the United States cannot exercise, and cannot claim, the rights of public war as against the people of a State in rebellion; in other words, sir, it has, at present, no *belligerent* right whatsoever."—*Vallandigham's Trial*, p. 205. This speech was prepared for the press by its author, so the extract given is absolutely correct. And the same doctrine has been asserted over and over again by this class of politicians,—the same class, mind! who are ever clamoring to their dupes with the feigned fear that the war-wielding power of this country is to override the Supreme Court of the United States, *whose decisions they pretend to accept as the final and absolute law!*

Yet, unknown to this advocate and to his client, full two months before this speech was uttered, the Supreme Court had unanimously, by all its judges, the much lauded Taney, C. J., concurring among the rest, decided, that, from July 13, 1861, according to the opinion of the minority, and from an earlier date, according to the opinion of the majority, the United States had been constitutionally, and in fact, carrying on a public civil war against the rebellious portion of the country, with the full belligerent rights which war gives, as known in the law of nations. Until the decisions embracing this doctrine appear in the regular Reports by Black, the reader will find them stated sufficiently at length in *Lawrence's Supplement* to his late edition of Wheaton.

But does the enunciation of this doctrine by the Supreme Court,—not by a heretical and fanatical majority of its judges merely, but by the whole court, including those staid and substantial members on whose shoulders even the church herself had heretofore reposed,—abate the denunciations of these men against the government? Are they ready to bow before their own authority, when this authority steps out from supporting them in their attempts to break down the people's respect for the government? — in their attempts to make prejudiced men believe, that, unless they elevate *them* to office, the Constitution will be overthrown? No! The more desperate the chances become of getting office by opposing the operations of the government in this trial hour, the more boisterous grows the clamor. And now, while I write, there are office-seeking demagogues trying to plunge the North into a civil war, not because the government is doing any thing which the Supreme Court has said it has no right to do, but because it does not set *them* up as the interpreters of the Constitution; and, in obedience to their interpretation, virtually stop the war.

So, then, according to these men, neither Congress, nor the President, nor yet the Supreme Court of the United States, is the proper interpreter of the Constitution; this work is to be done by politicians aspiring for office, and by newspapers in their interest catering to the prejudices of an unread rabble! One of the processes of the war — the draft, pronounced to be constitutional by Congress, by the President, and by those learned officers whom the Constitution has pointed out as the advisers of the President — must be stopped till the enemy has had time to overpower our reduced armies in the field, because demagogues deem it will promote their chances for an election to represent the draft to be unconstitutional! The demagogues, then, —

so they condescend to inform us themselves,— are the interpreters of the Constitution!

That the decisions which the Supreme Court has made, relating to the topics of the following pages, will please these men, I have no present belief. That they will bow before these decisions, I have no expectation, since they refuse to bow before the other decisions. But there is one thing to which they will bow. When the people throw off the demagogial trance into which they have been cast by office-seekers who want their votes and the votes of southern rebels at the same time, and so read for themselves the Constitution and the decisions of the Supreme Court, the most inveterate demagogue, *out of love to the people and the Constitution,* will eat his former words, and rush where the voters in heaviest column go.

CHAPTER II.

THE DIRECT CONSEQUENCES RESULTING FROM THE ACT OF SECESSION.

It has been assumed, even by men who are not Cursers of Ham, that, since the States seceding had no power to withdraw from the Union, therefore their several acts of secession were, in law, nullities; leaving the States to stand, toward the general government, in the same legal situation as if the acts had not been passed.

Let it, then, be stated, that this proposition has no foundation either in the law of the case or in the facts of the case. It is sustained by no decision of any court, by no *dictum* of any judge, by no observation of any writer on constitutional law; it rests only in mere loose assertion, made, since this rebellion broke out, by persons who, whatever might have been their capacity to form a correct opinion, had given to the question no adequate investigation. The phrase, "*The act of secession is a nullity,*" is, in most instances, practically employed for one or the other of two opposite purposes; either, to convey the idea, that the utterer of it is intensely loyal; or, on the other hand, to impress on the hearer's mind the falsehood, that no evil consequences can lawfully be made to fall upon the participators in secession, since the act of seceding is a null act.

Looking at this question as one of fact, we all know, every boy in the land knows, it is known even to the most ignorant peasant in Europe, that the proposition which asserts the act of secession to be a nullity is false. I say, everybody knows that secession was *not a nullity in fact*. Upon the act of secession, the State which had passed it, ceased to have a governor, judges, legislators, and other State officers, performing their several official functions under the recognized binding obligation of an oath to support the Constitution of the United States. No considerable number of the citizen-voters in any such State acknowledged, after the passage of the secession act, what all acknowledged before, a duty of allegiance to the United States; and, in no such State, did any single State officer, of any grade whatever, acknowledge, after the act was passed, such duty of allegiance. The relation of the State to the United States was, by the act, as completely changed, looking at the matter now simply as one of *fact*, as would have been the relation of the moon to the earth if she had gone off and embraced the sun, or as would now be that of my pen to this sheet of paper, if, ceasing to write upon it, its material substance should go down and incorporate itself with the sole of my boot. Completely, thus, did the act of secession change, *in fact*, the relation of each seceding State to the United States.

But if the moon should go and embrace the sun, there would be left on the earth men who would say, that, since this procedure was contrary to the law of nature, it did not take place *in law;* but, *in law,* the moon still revolves around our planet as before: so, should this pen incorporate itself into the substance of the sole of my boot, we should hear wiseacres tell, that this procedure was utterly forbidden by the law of its nature, therefore it did not take place, therefore the pen is writing still, — at least it is still writing *in law.*

Is, then, the relation of the seceded States to the United States one thing in fact, and directly the opposite thing in law? These States are, as they always were, bound, by law, to render allegiance to the United States; *it is a fact of the law* that they are so bound, — Do they, therefore, *render allegiance in law?* If yea, why is this war? If their relations are not changed in law, what has the law to complain of? And, pray tell, have we the right to fight a State, or a man, whose *conduct in fact* has wrought no change in *his relation to us in law?* So, in the jurisprudence of our courts, if I sue you, Mr. Reader, and it appears that, on a day named before suit brought, I had no right in law and in fact to sue you, yet I prove a change in fact to have taken place after that day, — Does this entitle me to recover unless the change brought also with it a change in our legal relations?

No. If it be true that secession has wrought no change in legal relations between the seceded States and the United States, then the United States has no legal right to complain of it. Complaint might, indeed, be made of such action of the people as capturing forts, marching armies against us, and the like, but *not of the act of secession*. And it is a general proposition, — a proposition to which, so far as I know or believe, there is no exception, — that *no man has any legal right to complain of any act which does not change the legal relation between himself and the doer of the act*. From this proposition comes another, or, rather, the other is the same proposition as this, put in different shape, and applied to the particular subject of our present discussion, namely, — *If secession has not changed the legal relation of the seceded States to the United States, then, as the United States has no legal right to complain, so these States had the legal right to secede*.

But, in truth, the act of secession did work as great a change in law as it did in fact. If it wrought no other change, it placed the seceded States in the situation of delinquents from duty, and placed the United States under obligation to come down upon them with all its power, military and civil. It annulled all those civil rights which they derived under the Constitution, and which pertain to the ordinary condition of peace; because such is the effect of war; and that the United States is now constitutionally carrying on against them, war in its full sense, with its full consequences, we have already seen to have been adjudged by the Supreme Court. I am speaking of the effect of the act of secession, and of the matter as it now stands, not of what will legally result from a return by these States to duty. Therefore, let me repeat, that, as already decided by the Supreme Court of the United States, the act of secession, with the war which has followed it, has placed the seceded States in the condition of a mere belligerent in war, as to rights, the United States being the other belligerent, — of war as known to the law of nations, — of war depriving those States, and their people, of the ordinary civil rights pertaining to peace, as set down in the Constitution. So, at least, I understand the decisions as I have seen them, not fully reported; and such is plainly the true view of the question. Furthermore, the act of secession brought upon the seceded States *those special consequences which the Constitution has provided as the penalty for the act.* What those special consequences are, we shall see further on in this chapter.

These are the outside, palpable views of the matter, and they require no further illustration. But there are also some inner views, which it will be well to consider here. It is known to every person in this country, whether read in the law or not, that, by the common understanding and by the practice in all the States, a State may change, as often as she pleases, her forms of State government, — a change which is usually effected by an alteration of her State Constitution, or the adoption of a new one, — only that this proposition has, somewhere, its limits. This general doctrine has been sanctioned by the Supreme Court in several cases; for the present purpose it will be sufficient to refer to *Luther* v. *Borden*, 7 How. U. S. 1, — a case which will be again cited a little further on.

When we inquire for the limits of this doctrine,

we find them drawn in the United States Constitution. One of these limits will be more particularly considered in the fourth chapter of this pamphlet, where it will be seen, that, if a State has entered into a contract, she cannot, by any change in her constitution, cast off the obligation of the contract, being restrained from doing so by the well-known clause in the Constitution of the United States, prohibiting the States from passing "any law impairing the obligation of contracts."

Another limit is, that, since by the Constitution of the United States the judges and other officers of the States must be sworn to support this Constitution, no State can so change her form of government as to be entitled to dispense with the administration of this oath to these officers.

Another limit, which has been much discussed in this country, is, that no State can, by any act of governmental change or otherwise, divest herself of the duty to return fugitives from labor, escaping within her borders from other States.

There are still further limits, but those which have been mentioned are sufficient for the present purpose of illustration.

Now, suppose a State attempts, by means of some change in her government, to free herself from one or more of the before-mentioned duties, or from any other particular obligation, or all the obligations, imposed on her by the Constitution of the United States, — What is the result, and what course is the general government to pursue toward her? Obviously the matter will depend somewhat upon the nature of the alteration in the State government attempted, and upon a consideration of the particular duty or duties designed to be evaded. But what is to be here noted is this: The political department of the general government may decline to recognize the new State government, in which case the declinature will be binding also upon the judicial department; or, this course not having been in the individual instance pursued, the several departments of the United States government will treat as null those things in the State government and constitution which are in conflict with the Constitution of the United States. Each of these two methods will be illustrated in the following pages of this chapter.

In the fourth chapter, the reader will see some decisions referred to, in causes which went for adjudication before the Supreme Court of the United States; wherein it appeared, that the State of Ohio had undertaken, first by a legislative act, and afterward by adopting a new constitution, to cast off from herself the obligation of a contract relating to the subject of taxation. Here, when she changed her constitution, no objection was interposed by the general government to the change; and so the new State government was recognized as the proper State government, standing legitimately in the place of the old one. But the Supreme Court held, that the change, though thus recognized in general terms by the political department of the government of the United States, could not be deemed judicially so to operate as to relieve the State from the obligation of her contract. Doubtless the political department, could the question have gone before it, as it did before the judicial, would have decided it also in the same way. Here, it is seen, the new constitution and government of Ohio were, up to a certain point, recognized and held to be good and valid for every thing they professed and claimed; but, beyond this point, to be mere null things, because in conflict with the Constitution of the United States. And this decision harmonizes with the general doctrine of the courts, respecting unconstitutional laws; namely, that a statute is to be adjudged constitutional for all purposes which it was within the constitutional power of the legislature passing the statute to effect; for all other purposes, void. It is seldom, therefore, that a legislative act is pronounced void in full; it is void so far as it transcends the constitutional power of the legislature passing it; for the rest, valid. And so likewise, we see, are the acts of a State changing her State constitution and government; they may be good in part, and invalid for the residue. Such an instance is shown in these cases from Ohio, decided, as just mentioned, by the Supreme Court of the United States.

But a State may undertake to make such a sweeping change in her government, that the United States authorities will refuse to recognize, to any extent, the new government. Such an instance, or series of instances, formed the prelude to the present war. Certain States called conventions, such as, according to established custom and law, were authorized to change the governments of the States; then, through these conventions, proceeded to disrobe

themselves of their State governments; next, to
enrobe themselves in new governments, unknown
to the Constitution of the United States. This, in
exact language, is what these States performed in
the act of secession. The first part of the process
— namely, the disrobing of themselves of the old
governments — was a proceeding fully within their
power; it was no violation of the Constitution of
the United States. But the remaining part of the
process — namely, the attempted putting on of disloyal robes — was a matter quite beyond their
power; it was a thing done in violence to the National Constitution. And the omission to put on
new loyal robes, the old ones having been lawfully
taken off, became now, under the circumstances, an
omission of duty, violative of the Constitution of
the Nation. Some of these States, indeed, seceded
by legislative act; but the particular method adopted
was an internal affair of their own, and the case is
to be considered the same as if the secession of all
had been by convention.

When this work was fully done, the seceded
States presented themselves to the general government, and asked to be recognized in their new garbs.
But the general government refused to recognize
them thus, not because there was objection to the
mode in which the new garb was put on, the objection was to the garb itself. In Missouri, the convention which was elected to consider the matter of
secession, and which would have passed the secession
ordinance, had it been possible to obtain a vote of
the majority for such a purpose, finding the legis-

lature of the State disloyal, abolished it and established a new but loyal State government in its place; and the government of the United States recognized this new government, and disowned the old one.

As matter of settled law, therefore, the seceded States had the right to cast off their former State governments. This they did; and this fact the United States has recognized. The old governments of these States no longer exist as facts; the power to stop their breath existed constitutionally in the States; the States have exercised the power; the government of the United States has recognized the fact of its exercise; and, at this day, there are in these States no governments which are recognized by our general government. In other words, these States are, by our government, recognized as States having no State governments. And when we look into the case we perceive, that such they truly are.

Let us see a little further, how the matter stands with these States and the United States respectively. In the pamphlet entitled "Thoughts for the Times," I called attention to the following provision of the Constitution of the United States: Art. IV. § 4,—"*The United States shall guarantee to every State in this Union a republican form of government*, and shall protect each of them against invasion; and, on application of the legislature, or of the executive (when the legislature cannot be convened), against domestic violence." And we saw, that these seceded States have not, since secession, republican forms of government, within the meaning of this provision;

in fact, we now see, that they have no governments whatever, as recognized by the government of the United States. The inquiry, as to what is the precise meaning of the expression "republican form of government," as used in this constitutional provision, is therefore wholly unimportant here; because, when our United States government, acting correctly, recognizes the non-existence of any State government within a State, this recognition settles the main point, namely, that, since there is no government in the State, there is no "republican form of government" there. To say that a State has a republican form of government, when it has no government whatever, as recognized by the United States, would be the height of absurdity.

The United States is, therefore, bound to execute this guaranty of a republican form of government to the seceded States. As to the meaning of this provision, let me say a further word. The term "United States" is broad enough to include all the people of the United States, and all branches of its government. So, in fact, it does; but, in the case mentioned some pages back, of *Luther* v. *Borden*, 7 How. U. S. 1, which was a case growing out of what was called the Dorr rebellion in Rhode Island, the Supreme Court considered, that, though this clause of the United States Constitution did bind all the departments of the government of the United States, yet it was for the executive and legislative departments, — in other words, for what is called the political department, — not the judicial, to determine whether a particular State had, at a particular time, "a republican form of government," within the meaning of this provision; and, if there were within the State two such forms claiming to satisfy the provision, to decide which one of the two should be accepted as the true one, and the decision would bind the judicial tribunals. Let me quote a few of the words employed by Taney, C. J., in giving the opinion of the court: "The Constitution of the United States, as far as it has provided for an emergency of this kind, and authorized the general government to interfere in the domestic concerns of a State, has treated the subject as political in its nature, and placed the power in the hands of that department." The learned judge then recites the article of the Constitution which I have extracted just above, and proceeds: "Under this article of the Constitution it rests with Congress to decide, what government is the established one in a State. For as the United States guarantee to each State a republican government, Congress must necessarily decide what government is established in the State before it can determine whether it is republican or not. . . . Its decision is binding on every other department of the government, and could not be questioned in a judicial tribunal." The learned judge, however, goes on to show, that, in connection with Congress, the President has power also to participate in this decision; but, in no case, is the question one for the courts, the political department of the United States government always determines whether the government of a State is republican, within the meaning of the United States Constitution, and executes, or leads the way for executing (I give here the meaning, but do not use the exact words of the court) this guaranty.

I might quote also, if it were important, from the writings of the late John C. Calhoun, and show, that this judicial exposition of the Constitution is in accordance with his understanding of the provision, and of the respective duties, under it, of the political and judicial departments of the government. He even puts the case of Congress determining, in a time of profound peace, and no rebellion existing in any State, that the State constitutions under which slavery is maintained are, by reason of their maintaining it, not republican, thereby abolishing the institution in the States; and he explains to his readers, that, though this decision by Congress would be really a decision surpassing the power of this body, under these circumstances, yet still it would be binding on the courts, and the wrong would be without a remedy, — except, indeed, his great remedy of *nullification;* or its later form, secession. 1 *Calhoun's Works*, 332 et seq. In fact, the point is too plain, especially since the judicial opinion in *Luther* v. *Borden* was pronounced, to permit the mind of any person read in such questions to doubt. But the reader will see, as we go on, that the act of secession has so changed the circumstances, and the relations subsisting between Congress and the seceded States, as not only to authorize, but to require, Congress to effect, in those States, the same abolition of slavery now, which Mr. Calhoun properly held would be without remedy through the courts, were the thing so done, even in an ordinary time of peace, while the States were performing their full duties under the Constitution.

Now, as already observed, — for the reader must bear with me though I here indulge in repetition, — when the rebellious States seceded, they claimed, — so we all remember, — that the government of the United States should recognize them as independent powers, and their new State governments (for such, in fact, they were, whether there was any change in the individual persons holding the offices or not) as the true governments of those States. This claim the government of the United States refused to acknowledge. Yet it did recognize the fact, that these new governments, within those States, were not such governments as were contemplated by the Constitution of the United States. Whether, *as an abstract question*, they were republican or not, the government of the United States neither knew nor cared; it did know, that it did not accept them as *the* "republican forms of government" which were guaranteed to them in the Constitution. The department of our government which determined this question, in the first instance, was the executive; and, at the time when it was thus earliest determined, the presidential chair was occupied by a Democrat. Afterward the same matter was determined in the same way, by our present President, a Republican. Next, the legislative department followed the executive, deciding also the question in the same way in which the executive had decided it; the courts followed still on in this same path; and the whole loyal people accepted these several determinations as just; so that there are no persons and no powers in the country, except the avowed rebels and their official functionaries, by whom this, which I am now showing, is denied, either as matter of law, or as matter of fact. Except? No! there is no exception. The rebels do not deny this; they admit, as freely as do we, that their present State governments are not *the* "republican forms of government" meant by this section of the Constitution; they claim that they are not; they and we are here agreed.

We come once more, then, to the conclusion, no one contradicting, that there are not, in any of the seceded States, those republican forms of government which the United States, in the Constitution, guarantees to the several States. I have shown, because I wished to present the exact legal condition of the matter, that the States acted within their constitutional powers in casting off the old governments, but did not do their constitutional duties in declining to reclothe themselves in proper new ones. Whether the former clause of this proposition is correct or not, the fact stands, that there are not, in the seceded States, any governments which are, or ought to be, recognized by the government of the United States as State governments, within the meaning of the national Constitution. But the national Constitution provides, that the United States shall guarantee such governments to all the States; wherefore the effect of the act of secession was to place the seceded States under liability to be reclothed by "the United States," according to the terms of the Constitution.

In the pamphlet entitled "Thoughts for the Times," I showed, still further, what is the operation of this constitutional provision. I do not mean to repeat what I there said. But let me add, that, whether the view taken there and here is correct or not, *as regards the effect of this particular provision*, yet it is the view which has all along been entertained by what is deemed the sound and conservative part of our loyal community, *as deducible in some way from the Constitution*.

Let me explain. During the session of Congress which immediately preceded the last (1861-2), Mr. Sumner of Massachusetts brought forward, in the form of resolutions, a proposition before the Senate, that, in effect, the seceded States be deemed to be, and held as, territories. This, at all events, is what the resolutions were understood by most people to mean. But lo, what a storm! The sound and conservative men, the men who had escaped the poison of radicalism and fanaticism, the writer of this pamphlet among the rest (for I am a conservative, and no radical or fanatic), *condemned the resolutions as amounting to a proposed infringement of the Constitution of the United States*. We all deemed, that it would violate the provisions of this instrument to deprive the seceded States of their condition as States, and compel them to assume the lower status of territories; thus overwhelming those persons in these States who had not participated in the rebellion, and overwhelming unborn and unsinning children, in the common doom which properly enough follows treason, simply because the majority of the people had chosen for themselves the traitor's part. We agreed, that, for the protection of the innocent, the Constitution had guaranteed to these States, not to the traitors in them, governments within the Union, the same as though the majority had not rebelled. Perhaps Mr. Sumner was of the same opinion, and his idea was only to use the territorial governments as a means to execute the guaranty; but, be this as it will, all of us of the conservative class were distinct in this one voice, that the proposition was contrary to the Constitution, which, in our judgment, bound the United States to establish in the seceded States, not loyal territorial governments, but loyal State governments. Now, I do not know how others wrought out this conclusion of constitutional law, but I derived it from the clause we are here discussing. Whether the great conservative mass who agree with me, get it from the same clause or not, there is no need we should inquire; for the result is the same, come it from one clause or from another. *We all agree* — all but the radicals and fanatics — *that the United States, in the prosecution of this war against the seceded States, is bound to secure to those States republican State governments under the Constitution of the United States.*

But, as I showed in my "Thoughts for the Times," the former white voters of those States have refused, in mass, to carry on such governments. The refusal was earliest expressed in their several acts of secession; and, although the white voters did not all concur then in those acts, but a minority of considerable dimensions opposed, this minority afterward gave to them an almost unanimous consent and ratification. For example, the present Vice-President of the Confederacy stood manfully up in opposition at first, but he afterward yielded to the secession act of his State his cordial support; and his case is but the case of almost all those who constituted the original minority.

Now, there can be no State governments, republican in form, carried on in these seceded States, except by willing voters. It would be a mockery to say, that the republican governments which we seek, and which the Constitution demands, for these States, are governments in which Jeff. Davis and the rest shall be forced up to the polls as prisoners of war, and compelled, at the point of the bayonet, to deposit their votes. Therefore we are bound to accept such persons, dwelling on the soil, as, under the Constitution of the United States, can be made by Congress legally competent to carry on State governments, and such as have not declined to carry them on, by voting for secession or otherwise sustaining the secession cause; we are bound to make them, by congressional act, competent,—which, of course, implies, that they shall be set free, if before held as slaves;—and to empower them to establish State governments in these States. In determining who shall be accepted for the purpose, reference cannot be had either to the former or the present State laws; for State laws, even the laws of States which have not seceded, are never of any effect, and never to be regarded, as standing in opposition to the execution of any provision in the Constitution of the United States. This is a principle so familiar, that it does not need, for support here, any citation of authorities; probably there is scarcely a single volume of decisions by the Supreme Court wherein there are not cases sustaining this doctrine. Everywhere it is received as unquestioned legal truth, that the Constitution of the United States, and the statutes passed by Congress in pursuance of constitutional authority, are supreme over State constitutions and State statutes; and that Congress, when it pleases to act on any power conferred in the Constitution, — see *McCulloch* v. *Maryland*, 4 Wheat. 316, to be referred to again in our next chapter, — is to pursue the power in its own way, without regard to what may be the law, or may not be the law, prevailing in any particular State, or in all the States. Especially, when Congress is to take the initiative in establishing a State government in any State, this body must, of necessity, determine, as a first step, so much concerning what shall be the status of the people of the State as shall settle the question of their authority or want of authority to vote or otherwise act as participants in the government; for, without this, there can be no proceeding practically taken in the State in pursuance of the action of Congress, the question of who shall proceed in any matter being essentially involved in the direction that the matter be proceeded in. It is of the very essence of the direction by Congress in this case, that Congress shall fix the status of the negroes as free or slave; and, indeed, the status must be established as that of freedom and not of slavery, in order to furnish the material for erecting State governments where the whites have refused to carry on such governments. *This material is, in fact, the material presented by the States themselves.* Congress cannot ignore it; though, if there were other material presented in any sufficient and appropriate measure, Congress might, perhaps, select.

In respect to the seceded States, this proposition that State laws shall not stand in the way of an act of Congress carrying out a provision of the United States Constitution, is true also for a still stronger reason than the one above given. We have already seen, that, in these States, there are no State governments, as recognized by the United States. Thence it necessarily follows, that there can be, in these States, *no State laws as recognized by the United States.* These States stand, as we have seen, in the condition of a belligerent toward the United States, for as such only has the rebel power been recognized by the United States; but, even as such, there is a difference between them and an ordinary belligerent in a war between two independent nations. When two nations, which have recognized each other's existence as nations, enter into a war against one another, they do not ordinarily withdraw that recognition; but, constitutionally and lawfully, the United States declines to recognize the Southern Confederacy as a nation; declines, also, to recognize the existence of State governments in the several States of this Confederacy; therefore, she necessarily and constitutionally declines to recognize the existence of any law there,— other than, perhaps, such laws of the Union as are applicable to the circumstances, — except the law which attaches to the people as a belligerent.

Ridiculous would it be, then, to say, that the United States shall be obstructed in carrying out the provision of the Constitution under which this supreme power guarantees to States, so situated, the reëstablishment of republican governments, by some present, or past, or supposed future law assumed to exist in those States, standing there as a matter of internal State regulation!

There are, in all departments of life, disagreeable, as well as agreeable, duties; and the true philosopher takes life as he finds it, and is thankful alike for the bitter and for the sweet. There are disagreeable, as well as agreeable, constitutional duties; and the true patriot performs the one and the other class with equal alacrity, if not with equal love. We of New England remember, that our departed Webster used often to speak of this; and when some fanatical heretics, who did not pay due respect to the church of the Cursers of Ham, showed a disposition to disregard also their duty to the Constitution in the matter of returning fugitive slaves, he admonished them, that, though it was disagreeable to send back to his master a runaway negro, this was still a constitutional duty, which should be done with alacrity.

So in the matter now under consideration: the free whites of the seceded States have declined to carry on governments under the Constitution of the United States, but the enslaved blacks have not declined; and, as the Constitution requires us, not to reduce these States to territories, but to give them republican governments under the Constitution, we are compelled, therefore, either to take the blacks, or to refuse obedience to the Constitution. This is a disagreeable predicament; we Cursers of Ham must either permit these children of Ham, upon whom our curses have fallen, to exercise the duties of freemen, or else we must turn and curse the Constitution of our country likewise, and trample it in the dust. Hitherto it has been apparently the decision of Congress to do the latter; because, though there have been three sessions of Congress since the rebellion broke out, yet at no one of these sessions has there been any statute enacted, providing for the establishment of these new State governments within the seceded States. At the same time it must be acknowledged, that, though the President issued some proclamations pointing toward, if not looking at, an ultimate performance, at some future period, of constitutional duties in this matter, Congress did not nullify those proclamations by any act or resolution, wherefore she gave to them her implied consent. And perhaps there are some provisions of Congress respecting colored troops and the like, which provisions amount almost to express consent.

Still it is true, that hitherto Congress has steadily refused to do its full constitutional duty in this matter. I do not say, that there was not excuse for this refusal; the country was very reluctant to allow this duty to be done; "it was the proper business of members of Congress," said the newspapers and the people, "to attend to the crushing out of the rebellion, and not agitate such foolish questions as whether the supreme law of the land shall be obeyed by the supreme legislature of the land, or not. What virtue was there in obedience? Not any," answered most; but it was pretty well agreed, *that there was virtue in dissemble.*

As Peter once, under a strong temptation, denied his Lord and Master, so did we, Cursers of Ham, under a temptation equally strong, deny our dear Master Slavery. We wanted the votes of sinners, we wanted their good opinion, and we wanted a proper *status* from which to enforce the doctrines of our church. So we declared, that this blessed institution of slavery, this institution of our church, this rock whereon the church is built, was, as we deemed, an evil and a bad institution; and that — O Master Slavery! wilt thou ever forgive us? — we should gladly, if we constitutionally could, do away with it in the seceded States! But we said, and kept our hardened faces unchanging like marble when we said, that the Constitution forbade us to do such a thing, and that we loved the Constitution, and that we meant to obey the Constitution! We said, that the act of secession was a nullity; some of us added also, that the act of war was a nullity; and all of us bleated out, like innocent lambs on the mountains, that, therefore, the general government had no more power to abolish slavery in the seceded States now than before secession and war came on!

When, in years gone by, some of the heretics showed a disposition not to assist in the constitutional duty of returning fugitive slaves to their masters, they said, that the supposed law under which they were required to act was in violation of the Constitution of the United States. But they were readily answered, that the Supreme Court of the United States had pronounced the law to be constitutional, therefore the people were bound to accept it as such. Mr. Webster in his famous 7th of March speech said, that, in his judgment, the statute of 1850, about to be enacted, was in violation of the Constitution, but, as the judges of the Supreme Court thought otherwise, though he did not agree with them, he should vote, against his judgment of the Constitution, for the measure, and he did vote for it.

So now, we Cursers of Ham may think, some of us do think, as matter of private judgment, that nothing can be constitutional which goes against the tenets of our church. According to this view, this matter of cursing Ham is a thing above all other things in this land; any thing in the Constitution which interferes with the cursing, is to be taken as null; the high religious obligation binds in war the same as in peace; and, as Napoleon chose to be whipped, sneaking, like a spaniel, out of Russia, rather than receive the help of the serfs of Russia; and, as Pharaoh chose to be overwhelmed, with all his host, in the Red Sea, rather than suffer his bondmen, the Israelites, to have their liberty; so are we bound, by this same higher law of our religion, as Cursers of Ham, to let the blood of our white sons flow out like water, to see the life of our country drowned in an unsuccessful war with this rebellion, to give up every thing we hold dear as citizens of what was erewhile a great Republic, rather than pause, even for a moment, in our divine work of cursing Ham. In other words, we hold, that it would be a violation of the Constitution — the Constitution of our saintships — should we now stop cursing.

But the Supreme Court of the United States has decided otherwise; therefore we may listen to the admonition of our Webster, speaking to us from his grave, and saying, — "Cast away your private judgments, take the interpretation which the Supreme Court has given; and, should this interpretation place you under obligation to perform a disagreeable constitutional duty, still you should discharge the duty with alacrity, if not with delight." I do not propose to enter, in these contracted pages, into a minute consideration of the decisions; should I do so, I should here perform the work, which, as I have already stated, I intend for a book, wherein, as it will embrace a wider range of subjects than does this pamphlet, the authorities can be so set as to shed, upon each particular point, an ampler and clearer light than can be made to radiate here.

First, then, the Supreme Court has decided that the political department of the United States government — namely, the President and Congress — is to determine what government within a State constitutes the "republican form of government" guaranteed in the Constitution. It is for this political department to recognize, or refuse to recognize, a particular government, within a State, as the true State government, and the courts are bound to follow its decision. In support of this proposition, I need only refer again to the case of *Luther* v. *Borden*, 7 How. U. S. 1.

In the next place, the Supreme Court, in the decision just mentioned, and in other decisions to which it is not necessary I should here particularly refer, has given its full judicial sanction to the legal fact of the binding obligation, upon the nation, of this clause of the Constitution guaranteeing republican governments to the States. We have here a perfect "squelcher," to use a not very elegant word, for all fanatics who would take away from the seceded States their right to remain States, and to keep within their borders such persons, who have not rebelled, as can be made voters, and to carry on in the future republican State governments.

In the next place, the Supreme Court has decided, that, for a person to be a voter within a State, under a State constitution, it is not necessary he should be a citizen of the United States. The common instance is that of unnaturalized foreigners, who are voters in some of the States. There are more cases than one sustaining this point. I need only refer here to one; it is a case in which the matter in respect to negroes was particularly considered. There has been some discrepancy of opinion, as to whether, in the absence of legislation by Congress on the subject, negroes born in this country, either originally as slaves or originally as free, are, when not held in slavery, entitled to be deemed citizens under the Constitution of the United States. Perhaps the weight of judicial authority may sustain the point, that they are not so entitled; at least, let it be so assumed for the purposes of this argument. In the famous Dred Scott case (*Scott* v. *Sandford*, 19 How. U. S. 393), the majority of the court were of opinion that they were not citizens; though, on the other hand, it is said, that this question was not necessarily involved in the case, therefore that the words used by the majority amount to no more than *dicta*, and do not constitute adjudged law. However this may be, the question was not raised, and could not be raised, as to what would be the effect of an act of Congress declaring the negroes of a particular State to be citizens of the United States. Yet the material matter is this, that, while the minority of the judges deemed free negroes to be citizens, at least in some cases, the majority agreed with the minority in this, that, in the language of Taney, C. J., who delivered the opinion of the majority, — " He [the free negro] may have all the rights and privileges [including the privilege of voting] of the citizen of a State," p. 405, provided the State chooses to give them to him. "For," continues the judge, " previous to the adoption of the Constitution of the United States, every State had the undoubted right to confer on whomsoever it pleased the character of citizen, and to endow him with all its rights. . . . . Nor have the several States surrendered the power of conferring these rights and privileges, by adopting the Constitution of the United States. Each

State may still confer them upon an alien, or any one it thinks proper, or upon any class or description of persons." Therefore, of course, in those cases in which Congress is called upon to determine who shall be the voters of a State, in organizing a new State government, it may exercise this discretion; doing, when it thus acts instead of the State, whatever the State might do if acting for herself; the same as Congress has sometimes done, in allowing, for instance, aliens to vote in the territories, both in the carrying on of the territorial government, and in the elevating also of the territory into a State.

In the next place, the Supreme Court, like all the other judicial tribunals, recognizes the obligation of law as more binding and authoritative upon the citizens and upon the government, — especially if the law is that supreme law which is called the Constitution, — than are the peculiar religious tenets of any sect. Though the Cursers of Ham may know, in their consciences, that in the presence of Him who is no respecter of earthly potentates or earthly rulers of any kind, the faith of the Cursers sits supreme over the Constitution, having the right to control it and all things else pertaining to this country, still the Supreme Court and the other courts hold themselves bound by the lower law of the Constitution in administering justice, notwithstanding the Cursers, whom the judges all respect, pay their superior allegiance to the higher law of the Church. Consequently, though a Curser may know, in his conscience, that a negro is not fit to be a voter, the

Supreme Court knows it not; it has laid down, as the law of the land, directly the opposite proposition.

In the next place, while the Supreme Court acknowledges, as do all the other courts, that, in proper circumstances, Necessity shall be received as giving the law,—or, in other words, that the rule of necessity is sometimes, because there can be no other rule, the rule of law,—yet the Supreme Court never accepts the doctrines of the Cursers, any more than the doctrines of the lower and less respectable sects, as furnishing the gauge and measure of the necessity which shall govern instead of the letter of the law. Therefore, though a Curser may not like to see negroes exercising civil rights, this being a thing contrary to the psalm of the whip, yet the Supreme Court, while it may regret that there should be any pauses in this psalm, feels still compelled to say,—"The psalm is not a thing which cannot be barred and stopped by the Constitution of the United States." The result of which is, that, as already seen, since the Constitution requires the United States to guarantee republican forms of government to the seceded States; since those States have not now any governments which the political department of the United States government has recognized, or can recognize, as coming within the terms of this guaranty; since the whites in those States have refused to carry on such governments; since the blacks have not refused; and since, *in law*, the blacks may, just as well as the whites, be empowered to execute the mandate of Congress for setting up the guaranteed governments there,— the Supreme Court cannot accept the peculiar religious tenets of the Cursers as a sufficient excuse, justifying a refusal by Congress to authorize the blacks.

In the last place, let it be impressed once more on the reader, that, since there are in the seceded States no governments, regarded by the United States as the State governments of those States, it comes within the adjudications of the Supreme Court, that Congress should not only settle beforehand the question of who shall be voters therein, to carry out its act for establishing new State governments there, *but what also shall be the principles on which those new State governments shall rest.* This latter course of legislation has been adopted, always with the approbation of the Supreme Court, when a State government was to be organized, for the first time, in a territory. Thus, when Louisiana was to be admitted as a State, the national legislature provided, by its act, both for the establishment of the new government, and for the insertion of certain specific matters in the constitution to be framed for the State; and the Supreme Court held, that the latter, as well as the former, lay within the congressional power. Said Catron, J., in delivering the opinion of the court: "All Congress intended, was to declare in advance, to the people of the territory, *the fundamental principles their constitution should contain; this was every way proper under the circumstances:* the instrument having been duly formed, and presented, it was for the national legislature to judge whether it contained the proper principles, and to accept it if it did; or reject it if it did not."

Permoli v. *The First Municipality of New Orleans*, 3 How. U. S. 589. Now, although I do not concur in the view, accepted by many persons, that, because there are no State governments in the seceded States, as recognized by the United States, therefore they are, in law, territories, to be held and governed as such, instead of being reclothed, under the guaranty clause of the United States Constitution, in new governmental State garments, — still it is palpable to me, as it must be to all, that the doctrine just cited, as held by the Supreme Court, applies to the case of these denuded States, crying through the guaranty clause for the new Union dress. If the seceded States are indeed territories, then, of course, the doctrine applies; if they are not territories, but are entitled to carry on State governments again, whether their claim of right to do so comes through this guaranty clause or through any other clause, or from any other source in or out of the Constitution, the doctrine equally applies. If, for any reason, these seceded States have not now governments within the Union, and if the United States has the right, whether coupled with the duty or not, to cause governments acknowledging allegiance to the Union to be established in these States (a point which the Supreme Court, as we have seen, has already decided in favor of my argument), then, whichever of these positions we take, conducting to the result that the present war is no violation of the Constitution of the United States, the doctrine of our decision applies to the case. And according to to this doctrine, — the doctrine of the Supreme

Court of the United States, — though Congress should not feel bound by the guaranty, as a matter of duty, to establish new State governments in the seceded States, still, in authorizing the establishment of such governments, it would be competent for Congress. I here employ the language of the court, "to declare, in advance, the fundamental principles their constitutions should contain;" and, in the further language of the court, this proceeding would be "every way proper under the circumstances." The direction, then, might be, that, under the new constitutions and governments, the negroes should be freemen, and not slaves. And since the negroes had assisted the United States in putting down the rebellion, some of them by active labors, and others by keeping quiet and abstaining from servile insurrection, which might rebound unfavorably against the cause of the Union, all in pursuance of the request of the United States government, as contained in the Emancipation Proclamation issued by the President, and in other acts and orders proceeding from competent authority, — since, I say, the negroes had done this under the promise of universal freedom in all but certain excepted parts of the seceded States, then, if Congress failed to provide, in establishing the new State governments, for the perpetuity of their freedom, thus repudiating the debt contracted with unread and confiding men, it would be also "every way proper, under the circumstances," for all the dwellers on the earth, having souls of honesty in them, to hoot and deride, and then to trample our nation out, as unfit to live beneath the sun!

The only matter, therefore, on which there is any room to hang a doubt, is, not whether Congress has the constitutional power to secure freedom to the slaves in the seceded States, but whether, had not the Emancipation Proclamation been issued, she would even then have any liberty to decline. As the question stands since the issuing of the proclamation, the only difference of opinion which can arise is, whether, if she now declines, she will, by the declinature, merely break the faith of the nation, or whether she will break also the Constitution. According to the view taken in these pages, it would be in the discretion of Congress to liberate the slaves or not, as a mere act under the Constitution upon any ordinary case of a State ceasing to have a State government; but, when the reason of this ceasing was, that the whites had refused to carry on such a government, the circumstances lying outside the Constitution compelled Congress to accept the blacks, instead of exercising a choice between them and the whites, thus making the blacks free.

We see, therefore, what is the penalty provided in the Constitution for secession; it is, *that slavery be abolished in the seceding States.* These States voluntarily incurred the penalty,—Who stands forth to say, that it cannot be constitutionally inflicted?

It is not for me, with prophetic horn, to usher in the future, whether of weal or of woe. But if I were the most black-hearted fiend this universe contains, I could not call for a more damnable doom to fall on him whom I would torment, than I believe will be his doom, who, professing to be read in the laws of the land, stands now up with brazen face and declares, before a listening world and a listening and recording Heaven, that it would be right and just, and a thing in accord with the Constitution of our country, to proclaim a peace to the rebels of the South, based upon a continuation of the fact of slavery over those negroes of the South to whom the earlier Proclamation of our chief magistrate, issued with no dissent from Congress, promised the boon of freedom upon their remaining quiet during these weary months of war, and not rising against their masters. If any such man shall read these lines, let me say to him, not in the spirit of prophecy, for the scroll of the prophet is not given me to unroll, but in the more earthly spirit which discerns a common effect lying within its cause, that, whether there be in the hereafter a lake burning with fire and brimstone or not, there is, alike in the present and in the future, a Soul of the Universe which burns with a fire more consuming than the fire of brimstone, around those forlorn spirits, who, on earth, put out the false tongue to cleave to the ground the feeble ones who have no power to resist.

CHAPTER III.

SOME RADICAL VIEWS CONSIDERED.

The last chapter embraces a pretty wide view, and in some respects a complete one, of the doctrine, that, since the United States is lawfully undertaking to restore the seceded States to their old position of States standing clothed in State governments within the Union, — since it is the duty of the United States to restore them, — since the duty carries with it also the power, including the power over the means, — and since, in the actual facts existing, this power can be exercised only in the way pointed out in the last chapter, namely, as governments in States within the Union must be conducted by willing voters, as the whites in the seceded States are unwilling, and as the blacks are willing, by accepting the blacks, together with any whites who may not have expressed their unwillingness, and clothing them with the needful authority, — therefore the law (I am not speaking now of the theology of the Church of the Cursers), *the law* requires the United States thus to accept and authorize these blacks, and these few loyal whites.

Whether this doctrine be derived from the clause in the Constitution guaranteeing to the States republican forms of government (interpreted to mean such republican governments as the Constitution of the Union has particularly prescribed for the States), or whether the duty of restoring to these States such governments be found in some other clause, or gathered from the entire instrument, or drawn out from among those general principles of government which lie outside of the instrument — this is immaterial to the argument; the result is the same, be the origin of the obligation, or the right, one thing or another thing. I have traced the doctrine, the duty, the obligation, the right, whatever we may call it, to the clause mentioned, because I believe this to be its true source; yet I wish also to impress the reader with the other truth, that, should I be found to be mistaken in this, not one grain will thereby be lifted from the weight of the main argument. The United States is now engaged in a war, holden by the Supreme Court to be a constitutional war, waged for the purpose of bringing back the seceded States into the Union. The Constitution, therefore, to put the matter in its mildest way, authorizes the carrying on of the war by such means as the circumstances of the case show to be available for the attainment of the end. The end is the actual exercise of the elective franchise in these States by willing voters; who are willing, who are unwilling, we all know. Shall we, then, take the willing, and thus reasonably exercise the right? Or shall we refuse to accept the willing, while we fight the unwilling, and thus spurn the very thing we seek?

But if this war is a lawful war, it is a war also accompanied with a *duty*. No nation can lawfully enter into a war, unless duty leads the way. This nation is, therefore, under obligation, under the obligation of duty, — consequently under the obligation of *law*, either the law of the Constitution, or the law of nations, or the law of nature, — under the obligation of some kind of recognized law, to carry on this war; and all but fanatics agree, that the sought-for end of the war is the establishment, in the seceded States, of State governments whose officers shall be sworn to support the Constitution of the United States, and shall be elected by willing voters. Who in these States are willing, who are unwilling, we all know. Shall we accept the willing, and thus discharge our legal duty? Or shall we reject the willing, while we fight the unwilling?

It is familiar truth, that every community, large or small, is divided into essentially two different classes of people. The one class is composed of those who cling to the established law, to what has been laid down and walked upon before; the other class, of those who are ever attempting something new, under the hope of making the future better than the past. The former class are called conservatives; the latter, radicals.

The reader has already seen, in these pages, that, whichever class is really the nearer right, the writer belongs to the class of conservatives. I cannot see the utility of unloosing the fixed and the stable, which we have always deemed to be the true, and taking in the place thereof something new, which is merely experimental, simply because some untried theory says it is better than the old. Therefore it is, that I hold to the duty of obeying the law of the land, the law as actually written and expounded by the governmental powers entitled to expound it, instead of breaking the law out of reverence to some glittering fancy, and upon motion of our own individual wills. And even where the law is to be changed, — for change is written on all things, both in the earth and in the sky, — I am still opposed to novel experiments, and the following of mere specious theories. In such a case, I would try no legal innovation, however fine. I would select, out of those laws which God has used ever since his creation rose into being, the particular law which suited the altered circumstances, and adopt it. Should I find that the law sought was embraced in some tenet of the Cursers, I would enact the tenet into law; but, until the tenet was so enacted, though I might, as a religious being, pay my vows to the Supreme One in the halls dedicated to the worship of God after the forms of the Cursers, yet, as a citizen of the United States, I should obey the existing law of the land, rather than the law which I supposed ought to exist; in other words, I should not set up the tenet above the Constitution of the country, as expounded by the Supreme Court.

Such as these are the reasons which lead me to urge upon the reader an exact attention to the law as it stands written, in distinction from the law which we, as Cursers of Ham, might wish to have written. I know, I cannot but feel at every stroke of my pen, that, in the present circumstances of the country, there is a deplorable want of harmony between the claims of our Constitution and the demands of our religion. It is not strange, therefore, that radicalism should clamor for the lifting up of the Church, and the putting down of the Constitution. The true view, however, is,—so, at least, the matter appears to me, who cannot see the blessings promised to flow from the establishment of radical doctrines,—that, inasmuch as the claims of religion should not be disregarded, the Church should invite into convention with her the whole sinning country, then, if she can convert the country over to her views, let a new Constitution for the country be adopted; but, while the old Constitution stands, let it be obeyed.

Still, as radicalism is the form of things which most prevails among us, I cannot well avoid giving, in this pamphlet, some space to the consideration of a few of the more prominent radical views. In my "Thoughts for the Times," I briefly spoke of the radicalism of the administration of the late President Buchanan, which administration set up some glittering theories, as to how the rebelling States were to be won back, in the place of obeying the law of the land which required, that the heavy arm of the nation's power should be laid upon the incipient rebellion to smother it before it had grown strong. I am now about to speak of what happened more under the direction of the Republican party. — that is, it seems to have so happened, simply because the Republican party was in power; but it was done with the concurrence also of the Democratic party, and in compliance with its demand.

It is this, that, as already observed, the national Congress failed, session after session, to provide for the establishment of new republican governments in the seceded States, in violation of the clause of the Constitution we have been considering, in consequence of some higher-law notions which seem to have pervaded that body and the public at large. Had there been a disposition simply to follow the law of the land, there would have been passed an act authorizing all persons in the seceded States, not disloyal to the general government, — including, of course, those who were theretofore held as slaves, — to organize, as fast as the President, who is commander-in-chief of the army, should deem prudent and practicable, new State governments in place of the old ones which the rebels had cast off.

But this course, though it was what the law of the Constitution required, was rejected; the reasons for the rejection being various.

Many, perhaps the majority, of those who participated in thus violating the Constitution, were undoubtedly influenced therein by their strong attachment to the doctrines of our Church of the Cursers. These persons may not have been openly members of the church; they may even have denied the church, as did Charles II. of England, who partook of its extreme unction only, and of this merely in private, when the world was shut out, and death and the priest were barred in with him. They may even have pronounced as many oaths against the Church of the Cursers as had Charles II. against the Church of Rome; for the crown of political demagogism in this country is office, — in the heaven which the church promises to her followers, all wear crowns, — and there have been lovers of the crown here, the same as in England. Where heretics vote, whether a man shall avow his church connection, or not, depends sometimes on the strength of his love of — *the crown*. But if the Cursers of Ham flourish as greenly in heaven as they do in this country, undoubtedly God, who pities the infirmities of his saints, will, when they get to heaven, and he sees the tear of repentance in their eyes, take it and therewith wash away the stain from their souls.

Another reason for the refusal to obey the Constitution was this: The fact was plain, that, whatever law should be enacted by Congress, it could not be carried into practical effect in the establishment of new State governments in the seceded States, faster than the victorious Union arms cleared the way for the work. Now, there were persons who said, — "Why should I obey the Constitution, unless I can see the uses of obedience clearly attendant upon the act?" And they thought, that, by putting off obeying long enough, they might perhaps escape the duty to obey altogether.

This form of radicalism is one of the most common forms; it is known in every country. With us, the business of Congress is to enact laws; the business of the army is to fight. And the private opinion of any man, that there will be no immediate use for a law which the Constitution requires Congress to enact, "because," saith the private opinion, "the army will not get through with its work of fighting until another Congress sits," is no legal answer to the legal duty to enact the law. I have already recognized *necessity* as excusing the performance of a duty; but here there is no necessity operating in the case. The rebel bayonets may obstruct the passage of the army, but they cannot obstruct the passage of statutes, so long as no rebel power holds a seat in Washington, and our law-makers do hold seats there. There can be no ranker radicalism than that which says: "My private judgment as to whether it will do any good to obey the laws shall stand in the place of obedience." When this kind of radicalism becomes universal, there is an end of all order, and anarchy is king.

"Then," says the radical, "let me shape the matter thus: Inasmuch as the seceded States are inhabited by men who have declined to carry on republican governments within the States, and by men who have not declined, I deem it to be best to direct, that the new governments shall be conducted by the former class, the same as were the old ones. When the former class are subdued," continues the radical, "they will be obliged to set up the new governments, and they will be more willing to do it if they can at the same time trample the latter class down as heretofore; therefore, as I must do something, I shall follow the dictate of policy, thus putting the rule back into the hands of the men who have renounced the right to rule, and followed up their renunciation by the commission of treason."

Well, I am inquiring after the law,— Will the radical tell me by what law, in this country, traitors are to be made office-holders and voters, and especially to the exclusion of men who have never been disloyal? I know there is such a thing as pardon, but any attempted remission which precedes or accompanies the offence is not pardon, it is license. Does the radical pretend, that it would be competent for Congress to enact as follows, — "Whoever commits treason in an attempt to destroy the Constitution and government of the United States, shall ever thereafter be deemed innocent of any offence, and shall still be entitled to all the privileges of an unoffending citizen?"

At the time, therefore, when the Constitution requires the enactment of a law for giving to the seceded States new State governments, those who led the States out of the Union, so far as States can go out, — that is, who denuded them of their former State governments under the Constitution, — are rebels in arms. Yet the radical says, "Let the law provide for making them the voters, and for excluding from the ballot, and even from personal liberty, those who have never rebelled."

Well, I cannot find any clause in the Constitution sanctioning such a procedure; I can find nothing in any decision of any judicial tribunal sanctioning it; nothing in the law of nations; nothing anywhere, unless it be among the mysterious and unwritten things belonging to our Church. On the other hand, such a procedure — I mean, of course, such a procedure taken while no pardon has gone out to the rebels — would be contrary to all the laws and all the usages of the civilized world; contrary to the reason of the case; contrary to the spirit of our Constitution; and contrary to any fact practicable, since it would be only providing that the rebels might do what they had refused to do, and *voluntarily vote under the United States Constitution at the point of the bayonet!*

"Then," says the radical, "one more course remains for me. There are a very few white persons in the seceded States who have not taken part in the general treason of the whites there. I will vote to organize an oligarchy in those States; making, in this new form of government, the few loyal whites the rulers both over the disloyal whites, and, with the title of master superadded, over the blacks also." This proposition sounds well, but it is not the proposition of the Constitution. By the Constitution, the United States is not to guarantee to the seceded States oligarchies, but republican forms of government. It might be doubted, as indeed it has been, whether, as an original question, any government is republican wherein a large proportion of the people are slaves; but, assuming, as I cheerfully do, that, under our Constitution, interpreted by the comparison of clause with clause, and by bringing the light of the circumstances in which it was formed to illumine the whole, such a government for a State may answer the description of "republican," as the word is used in the clause now under consideration, still the oligarchy proposed by our radical is a thing entirely different from this. The circumstances which shed the illuminating light now, are diametrically opposite to those in which the Constitution was originally formed. The illuminating other clauses point, in this instance, differently from what they do in the other; and there is a difference between a government carried on by a mere handful of the whites, and one carried on by the mass of them. If the government proposed by our radical is to be deemed, under the circumstances now existing, republican, then there is no such thing known on earth as a government which is not republican.

At the same time it must be acknowledged, that there is laid up among the mysteries of the Church of the Cursers, one gleamy, blessed tenet, out of which, when it is gently pressed, there flows something milky and white, bearing a resemblance to this white doctrine, as thus in-milked by our radical babe; and, in fairness, I cannot pass on without calling the reader's attention to it. Not easy is it for sinful speech to describe a thing so saintly; but I will try, and see what words can do on this occasion. Turning, therefore, this milky whiteness into speech, it flows thus: "A negro is an heir of heaven, but he cannot be an heir of earth; that is, though he can have a seat among the blest above, he has, in the language of the earthly law, no 'hereditable' quality below. Therefore a negro is a thing altogether of the sky; he is not taken into the 'account' here; he is not 'counted' here; he is heaven's 'treasure,' not earth's; he is to be considered as an outlaw below, for the glory of the negro is to shine above."

When this heavenly milk is turned into earthly law, the result is, that, according to the milk, a negro is nothing in law; therefore, though there should be in a State two hundred thousand loyal negroes, and twenty loyal whites, the case must be considered as though there were but twenty loyal persons, the negroes not being counted.

Now, whether, not counting the negroes, the twenty loyal whites could in such a case carry on what would amount to "a republican form of government," in a State, within the meaning of the phrase as used in the Constitution, I shall not here undertake to argue. And the reason why I do not, is, that, by the Constitution, *negroes are not nothings,— negroes do enter into the account,— negroes are counted.* That the radical babe is right, looking at the matter as one pertaining to the mysteries of the Church, I cheerfully concede; but the object of this pamphlet is to consider the question as one pertaining to the Constitution of the United States. Very difficult do I find it, so to separate the one from the other of these two things, as to enable the church members, among my readers, to look at the constitutional doctrines without having their eyes made at the same time blind by the simultaneous glare emitted from the tenet.

I would pause, and explain how it is, that, under our Constitution, negroes are not nothings, negroes are taken into the account, negroes count, and the like; but I cannot in this pamphlet say every thing which might be said, so, asking the reader to consult the Constitution for himself, I pass on.

Suppose the radical doctrines which I have thus far discussed in this chapter are all admissible, still they go only to show, that it is in the discretion of Congress, if its members please, not to give freedom to the slaves in the seceded States. The power to exercise the discretion the other way, and to grant this freedom, still remains.

And there is another point, which adds to the force of this. It has been said, and so often said as to have become wrought into the beliefs of many of the people as though it were a part of the Constitution, that the Constitution and government of the United States were made exclusively for white men, not at all for negroes. To me, I confess, it seems somewhat strange, that a Constitution and government should have been established on this continent for the benefit of a part only of the native-born people, on the one hand; and, on the other hand, for the benefit, in conjunction with this part, of all the people of Europe. Because it is a notorious fact, that, when any person comes here from Europe, he is, after a short residence, and a process of naturalization, entitled to substantially all the privileges flowing to the best class of citizens born in this country.

But not to debate this matter, supposing the proposition above stated to be correct, it follows, that our Constitution and government are grievously antagonistic to our great and honored Church of the Cursers of Ham. During most of this war, we have been giving the life's blood of the white part of our nation to be drank up by treason steel, in order that the negro might stand especially protected, and especially blest, under the folds of the Constitution. If the Constitution was not made for him, in God's name, why not let him be shot at and bayoneted, instead of my son or my brother? I had supposed that the Constitution was deemed to have been made,— such indeed is the doctrine practically enforced by the church, enforced under the penalty of its *anathema*, excluding him who should disobey from association with the sanctified *here*, and from the heaven of office *there*,— much more for negroes than for white men; else, why do we imperil the freedom of the whites in order that we may continue to the negroes the full blessings of slavery as of yore?

Not made for the negroes! Rejoice, all ye sons of Ham, the day which you seek for, but ought never to find, wherein you shall be free, has come! It was because we thought the Constitution was made for you, O Sons of Ham, that we were ready to pour out our money, our blood, our good name, our honesty, and our truth, to be licked up by the dogs of war, and by the whelps which guard the courts of the despots of the earth, rather than yield to the necessities of the times, and permit you to join with us in one common effort to subdue the foe of our country. So, when we said the Constitution *was* made for you, more than for the white man, and that we should violate it if we did not spurn you from the ranks of the free, we lied — did we? and the Constitution, after all, was *not* made for you!

Rejoice, then, O white men! If the Constitution

no longer requires us to give the blood and the treasure of the country to the work of keeping down the negroes of the seceded States, but leaves this to the care of the Church alone — rejoice! Whenever this proposition comes to be believed throughout the country, whenever it is generally understood in the loyal States that the Constitution was made solely for white men, and not at all for keeping negroes in bondage, not only will this war cease, but a brighter and happier peace will descend upon our country than she ever knew before.

Concede, then, that the Constitution was made solely for the whites, not at all for the blacks, and we have arrived at the conclusion to which I have been all along striving to conduct the reader. It still stands true, for só it has been decided by our highest tribunal, and by the practice of some of the States, that, for the benefit of the whites, negroes may be permitted to participate in carrying on State governments. For the benefit of the whites, then, they may spring up as freemen in the seceded States, and hold these States against the waves of treason. For the benefit of the whites, they may mingle their blood with the blood of the whites on the battle-field. And I hope I shall not be accused of any disrespect to those holy members of our Church of the Cursers, who, to preserve to the negroes' souls the blessings of the discipline of slavery on earth, are ready to sacrifice their own souls and the souls of their children on the altar of slavery, when I address an observation to another class, whose motives are not so pure. You, then, who so hate negroes that you are unwilling they should fight with us to preserve the freedom of our country of whites, on any terms which shall leave them free afterward, should rejoice that the negroes are not such graceless, brainless, scoundrels as yourselves! Should they not be willing to make themselves free, except on conditions which shall leave you slaves, where will you stand, where will our country stand, hereafter?

Men may say what they will in their moments of passion, yet every man of cool brain knows, that, if the negroes and the whites in the seceded States join hands, and the negroes do not come to our help, the permanent restoration of the Union is as impossible as it would be now to reach out and draw down the moon to mingle her masses with those of our earth. I am not speaking of what may be done by way of temporary conquests. I am speaking of a permanent restoration of the Union. And those few white men of the South whose love for the Union surpasses their love for the Church, know this truth quite as well as do you, Mr. Reader, or as I do. And when another class of the white men of the South, namely, those who, not possessing the heroism of martyrs, desire peace and worldly prosperity more than they desire either the prosperity of the church in her present unfoldings under the care of the rebel government, on the one hand, or the restoration of the Union, on the other hand, see the loyal country standing clearly, and, as they believe, immovably, on ground which shall attach to us the mass of the blacks of the South, and shall not put the present rebels into such a position as will enable them to domineer over either the blacks or the minority of the whites, — when, in short, they perceive that civil justice is to be administered in their States in place of the religious discipline of the Cursers, they will then, but not before, discover safety in a full and unreserved espousal of the cause of the Union.

It is not within the purpose of this pamphlet to enter into a discussion of questions of mere governmental policy; yet I cannot forbear adding to what I have just said, the one thought, that, if the restoration of the Union means simply the lifting up of the old stars and stripes to float over the temple of the Cursers, while the priests within still carry on, protected by the Union arms, the same baptism of blood which during these two and more years of the war has been filling heaven with the souls of true lovers of the Union, — what hope can now light up a Union man's face at the South, even though the face be white? Why should any white man there raise his hand against the powers which now be, if the only thing which the Union army is to effect is to change the print-block whereon an overhanging rag is to be made red? If encouragement is to be given to men at the South in espousing the cause of the Union, it must be in the form of some reasonable assurance of protection for the future. The northern branch of the Church of the Cursers demands the performance of a thing impossible, — impossible, because the two parts of the thing are directly repugnant one to the other; namely, that Southern white men shall be *encouraged* to espouse the Union cause, and that at the same time they shall be set where they see the power of their own neighbor-haters of the Union descending slowly and surely upon them to crush them to death!

I must mention one more point upon which radicalism, disregarding the law, has wrought much mischief. It is this. The law, as all who are familiar with such matters know, provides, that, as stated in brief in the last chapter, whenever a discretionary power is given to a man, or to a body of men, the man or the men who are to exercise the power, in distinction from any third person or persons, must determine the mode of its exercise. In pursuance of this principle, it is held by the Supreme Court, that, when Congress would act upon any power conferred upon this body by the Constitution of the United States, it is for Congress to select her own methods whereby she shall carry out the power. For authority sustaining this position, see, among other cases, *McCulloch* v. *Maryland*, 4 Wheat. 316. This is the case in which the Supreme Court held the Bank of the United States to be constitutional; and, although the opinion did not satisfy the judgment of the entire country upon the main point, I am not aware that any doubt was entertained of the correctness of this proposition, which is mere matter of familiar law. Said Marshall, C. J., speaking for the whole court: "The government which has a right to do an act, and has imposed on it the duty of performing that act, must, according to the dictates of reason, be allowed to select the means." If this privilege of selection were not given to it, but to another, the other might, by refusing to select, defeat the act. So if our seceded States, speaking through the same voters whose mandate was executed in the passage of their secession ordinances, were to select the means whereby Congress should clothe them anew in State governments under the Constitution of the Union, how long, pray, would they be in making the selection? And, as they have not selected, shall Congress wait, or select for them?

The radical says, "Let Congress ask, not the loyal people of the seceded States, but the same disloyal voters who took the States out of their position in the Union, to prescribe the time and the means by which these States shall be brought back; for," continues the radical, "I do not like the law which permits the party doing an act, in pursuance of a duty expressed in general terms, to do it in his own way. I think, that, if a thief is to be caught, the first duty of the officer put on his track ought to be to inquire of the thief, how and when he will please order the catching process to be executed."

Now, it does happen, that, in our free country, when a man has committed no offence against the laws, he goes and comes at his own pleasure; though, it is also true, that, if he has offended, he is to be caught by such means as the administrators of the laws may direct. There are persons who deem, that any catching of an offender is a wrongful violence done to his liberty. But I am not aware that any man has claimed, until our green young radical sprang up, since this war began, that it is the right of the thief to direct the steps of his pursuer, while at the same time it is the right of the pursuer to catch the thief.

Therefore, according to the law of the land, differing herein from those doctrines of the Cursers into which our green young radical has been just baptized, when Congress proceeds to execute the guaranty of a republican State government to seceded States, she is not to ask, before she takes her steps, those persons in the States who committed the act of secession, by what means the act shall be undone, but she is to choose, so far as she can, her own way. And she is, therefore, to determine which of the various forms of republican government known to our Constitution shall be established in these States. Were it not for the special facts of the case, she might, perhaps, elect that the new governments be those wherein slavery is protected; but, as we have seen, these special facts preclude her from this choice, since the only willing voters existing in any sufficient numbers are those who were formerly slaves; and, when they are intrusted with the duties of freemen, there is not left in the States the material out of which to make slaves; unless, indeed, the democratic doctrine of "rotation in office" should prevail, and the late masters should take their turn in sitting, in the place of the blest, under the droppings of the Cursers' sanctuary.

In ordinary circumstances, the people of a State proceed of their own motion to dress themselves in such republican garbs as they choose; hence we say, that they determine for themselves what their domestic institutions, as slave or free, shall be. But the case of secession is not the ordinary one; therefore in this case, as we have seen, since Congress is to take the initiative and dress the State, she, and not the seceding rebels, determines the kind of dress to be put on. Now, the green young radical here presents himself, grown into the full proportions of a bloated demagogue, and he speaks and says: "It is the established doctrine, fellow-citizens, that each State is to determine for herself what shall be her domestic institutions; therefore, shut your ears, fellow-citizens, do not listen to a fanatic who tells of the power of Congress to abolish slavery in the seceded States. Unless our southern brethren see, fellow-citizens, that we are ready to walk by the Constitution now, they will not, fellow-citizens, lay down their arms, and come up cheerfully and cast their votes for me for the next presidency, or for any one who will appoint me to office."

But why trace the windings of the snake, whose head is radicalism, whose tail is demagogism, and whose crooked betweens would be the sport of boys rather than men, did not men know that the snake is the scourge of the country? Adieu, then, to this part of my subject. In the following chapters, I shall look at the matter involved in this discussion, from other and different points of view.

CHAPTER IV.

THE EFFECT OF CONTRACT BETWEEN THE SECEDED STATES RETURNING, AND THE UNITED STATES.

The Constitution of the United States provides, Art. I. § 10, that "no State shall, without the consent of Congress .... enter into any agreement or compact with another State, or with a foreign power." There is no other clause of the Constitution which in any way impairs the right of the States to bind themselves by contract. An earlier part of this section, however, provides, that "no State shall enter into any treaty, alliance, or confederation; grant letters of marque and reprisal; coin money; emit letters of credit; make any thing but gold and silver coin a tender in payment of debts; pass any bill of attainder, *ex post facto* law, or *law impairing the obligation of contracts.*"

The result of these provisions is, that any State can enter into any contract which is not a "treaty," or other thing mentioned in the last quoted words; with this exception, that, if the contract is with another State of the Union, or with a foreign power, it must, to be valid, be accompanied with the consent of Congress. There have been several cases before the Supreme Court wherein these provisions were considered; suffice it, however, to say, that the right of the States to enter into contracts has been, in these cases, fully recognized; and thus made, if judicial decisions can add to the force of the plain letter of the Constitution, established law.

But while, with the exception just mentioned, the States can enter into contracts, they cannot, having entered into them, annul them. To do so would be to violate the clause declaring, that they shall not make any "law impairing the obligation of contracts." There are several cases bearing upon this particular question; but I need here refer only to a single series of them. The legislature of the State of Ohio passed, in 1845, a general banking act, wherein, according to the construction put upon the act by the Supreme Court of the United States, there was contained the provision, operating in the nature of a contract with the banks to be organized under it, that they should be subject to no higher taxation than a per centage of their profits therein mentioned. Afterward the legislature of Ohio, in the exercise of the great prerogative right of every State so to tax all property found within its dominions as to make the tax fully meet the expenses of the government, enacted a new tax law, under which these banks would have to pay a higher rate than the one specified in the original charter. This new law the Supreme Court of the United States held to be unconstitutional, as violating a valid contract made by the State with the banks. *State Bank of Ohio* v. *Knoop*, 16 How. U. S. 369. The Supreme Court of Ohio had deemed, that the provision in the charter did not amount to a contract such as would relieve the banks from a further tax if the necessities of the State so required; but, in the case just cited, and in subsequent cases, the Supreme Court of the United States adjudged otherwise, and enforced its own construction of what was claimed to be a contract. Finally the State of Ohio changed its *constitution;* and, by a new constitutional provision, imposed the higher tax on the banks. Yet the Supreme Court of the United States held, that the contract could not even in this way be got rid of; but that the constitution, as well as the statute, of Ohio, in so far as it impaired the obligation of the contract, was void. *Jefferson Branch Bank* v. *Skelly*, 1 Black, 436. See also *Franklin Branch Bank* v. *The State of Ohio*, 1 Black, 474. Here was an attempt, by the State, put forth first in the way of a legislative act, and afterward by a solemn change of the State constitution, to exercise, in opposition to its contract, the high sovereign right of taxation, a right which has no more been surrendered to the United States than has the high sovereign right to make slaves of men; yet the Supreme Court held, that there was a provision of the Constitution which reached the case, namely, the one which prohibited the State from impairing the obligation of its contract.

Therefore we may set it down as established law, established by the adjudications of the tribunal of highest resort, as well as by the plain language of the Constitution, that, when a State has entered into any contract, she cannot, even by a change of her constitution, annul the contract. It is binding upon her still, and the Supreme Court of the United States will so hold, whenever a case, involving the question, is brought before it.

If, therefore, one of these seceded States comes back into the Union, under an agreement entered into with Congress, that, in consideration of being thus received back, or in consideration of any remission of the penalty of treason incurred by any of her citizens, or in consideration of any thing else, she will thenceforward hold certain classes, or all, of her inhabitants to be freemen, the agreement becomes immediately binding upon her as a contract which, by no act, can she afterward impair.

There is no need that I should trace this matter out into any further detail. It is, I am aware, one of the religious tenets of our most respectable sect, the Cursers of Ham, that, should Congress undertake to do away with slavery in the present seceded States, those States could, Congress or no Congress, as matter of right, after returning into the Union, reëstablish it. Now, should Congress be so silly, or so addled by the doctrines of the Cursers, as to take back the States by acknowledging the new State governments, without this precaution of a contract with them, the cursing doctrine might prevail. I do not say it would, but that Congress would be very recreant to her duty did she not exercise the precaution.

CHAPTER V.

THE EMANCIPATION PROCLAMATION.

On the 22d day of September, 1862, the President of the United States put forth a Proclamation of which the following are the material parts:

"That on the first day of January, in the year of our Lord one thousand eight hundred and sixty-three, all persons held as slaves within any State or designated part of a State, the people whereof shall then be in rebellion against the United States, shall be then, thenceforward, and forever free; and the Executive Government of the United States, including the military and naval authority thereof, will recognize and maintain the freedom of such persons, and will do no act or acts to repress such persons, or any of them, in any efforts they may make for their actual freedom."

He then states, that on the first day of January next ensuing he shall issue another proclamation, designating the portions of the rebellious country to which this provision shall apply, and closes in the following words:

"And the Executive will in due time recommend, that all citizens of the United States who shall have remained loyal thereto throughout the rebellion shall (upon the restoration of the constitutional relation between the United States and their respective States and people, if that relation shall have been suspended or disturbed) be compensated for all losses by acts of the United States, including the loss of slaves."

The Proclamation contains some other matters not entering so directly as these into the subject of this chapter.

On the 1st day of January, 1863, the President put forth another Proclamation, in pursuance of the promise made in this one, whereof the material parts are as follows:

"I, Abraham Lincoln, President of the United States, by virtue of the power in me vested as commander-in-chief of the army and navy of the United States, in time of actual armed rebellion against the authority and government of the United States, and as a fit and necessary war measure for suppressing said rebellion, do, on this first day of January, in the year of our Lord one thousand eight hundred and sixty-three, and in accordance with my purpose so to do, publicly proclaimed for the full period of one hundred days . . . . order and designate the States and parts of States wherein the people thereof, respectively, are this day in rebellion against the United States, [to be] the following, to wit: Arkansas, Texas, Louisiana [with certain excepted parishes, including, as excepted, the city of New Orleans], Mississippi, Alabama, Florida, Georgia, South Carolina, North Carolina, and Virginia [excepting substantially that part of Virginia which has since been formed into the State of West Virginia, and Norfolk, with its neighborhood].

"And by virtue of the power and for the purpose aforesaid, I do order and declare that all persons held as slaves within said designated States and parts of States are, and henceforward shall be, free; and that the Executive Government of the United States, including the military and naval authorities thereof, will recognize and maintain the freedom of said persons.

"And I hereby enjoin upon the people so declared to be free to abstain from all violence, unless in necessary self-defence; and I recommend to them that, in all cases when allowed, they labor faithfully for reasonable wages.

"And I further declare and make known that such persons, of suitable condition, will be received into the armed service of the

United States to garrison forts, positions, stations, and other places, and to man vessels of all sorts in said service.

"And upon this act, sincerely believed to be an act of justice, warranted by the Constitution upon military necessity, I invoke the considerate judgment of mankind and the gracious favor of Almighty God."

These two proclamations are generally spoken of as one, — the Emancipation Proclamation, — and as such I shall speak of them in my further observations. The Proclamation was put forth at a time when our national cause had become very nauseous to the people and powers abroad. There was, in the first place, intense hatred to this country abroad; growing out, in part, of the fact that our civil and political institutions are not like those of Europe, and that the governing classes there fear their influence upon the opinions and conduct of the people whom they govern; and, in remaining part, out of the fact, that, until our secession war came, we seemed to be a very compact, while we were a rapidly increasing, power, — exciting the jealousy of rivalship in those who, in Europe, deemed themselves to be the true masters of the world. In the next place, there existed an intense anti-slavery feeling in Europe, and particularly in England; produced in part by a sincere belief, that the doctrines of the Church of the Cursers of Ham belonged to the class of spurious, and not of true, Christianity; and in part by the fact, that European despots had all along found it convenient to point to our slavery as showing the baleful effects of republican forms of government.

There were, therefore, real enemies and real friends to our country abroad. But when our country's friends abroad saw, that, while the South had made war in order to gain what she deemed to be a firmer base whereon to rear block after block, in addition to her former edifice of slavery, and to strengthen the hated edifice itself, the North, in giving back the proffered battle, showed as much regard for the old edifice as the South, and chose to run mighty risks of not succeeding rather than suffer the edifice to fall, they at first marvelled, then became disgusted, then vomited out their contempt. At this sick crisis in those who else would restrain the European governments from laying violent hands upon us, came the President's Emancipation Proclamation. It operated as a restorative to our else expiring friends in Europe; and, though it did not cure our enemies of their hate, it left them comparatively powerless for harm.

At home, the effect of the Proclamation was to strengthen some in the loyal cause, and to madden others. Those who, at the North, ministered to our great Ebon Deity in the Temple of the Cursers, — why, they were not mad, because saints never get mad; but holy wrath boiled within them, and the incense — that is, the steam — went up! Fanatics, not of the church, gave thanks to God; and Ham danced in his shoes.

But the genuine politicians were as cool as cucumbers in August. Those who partook of the "supper" in the inner holy place of the Church of the Cursers went out and said: "This sacrilegious act of the President so violateth the Constitution of the country, that it hath become the duty of all true patriots to leave off fighting the enemy of the country, and go to fighting the President." On the other hand, there were other politicians, not so holy as these, who said: "Let this act of the President stand for the present, it has saved us from a foreign war; it will delude the negroes into helping us, for they are no brighter than are our white friends abroad; and, when we have put the rebels down, we can then repudiate the Proclamation, and put down the negroes and the fanatics together!" The former class of politicians were connected chiefly with the Democratic party; the latter, with the Republican. There were in both parties men who were not politicians, and other men who were politicians of less unction than these. In both parties, and especially in the Republican, there were many more — I trust, amounting to the large majority of the people connected with each of the parties — who recognized as true the proposition, that public faith is better kept than broken, even if the faith has been pledged without the previously-obtained sanction of the Church.

Yet it is but a little while ago I saw, in a newspaper, an article copied from a very leading journal of the Republican party, in which the editor asserted, in the most confident language, that there was no considerable number of people in the Republican party who were not willing to repudiate the public faith pledged in the President's Proclamation, and restore all the slaves to their former status of slavery, if the seceded States could be induced, on these terms, to come back! He said (what is true, and properly true), that the war was not carried on by the general government to promote emancipation; therefore (what is not properly true), that the government ought to repudiate its debt of promised freedom, contracted in subduing the rebellion, whenever the seceded States expressed a willingness to return to their allegiance, on the basis of such repudiation. He told his readers, that he should like to see the man who would have the hardihood to step forward and object to this proposition; such a man, should one be found, would be quickly branded and hooted down!

This editor, let me suggest, should at once lay by the quill editorial, and enter into the service of the government as a negotiator of loans. Should he be able to impress capitalists with the idea which he strove to impress on all his readers, that, since this war is carried on, not to pay debts, but to subdue the rebellion, there is no man, unless he be some insignificant outcast from the Church, who would not urge the government to embrace the Jeff. Davis doctrine of repudiation, as the foundation whereon the Union should be restored, whenever Davis and his companions could be made willing to agree to these terms,—surely the ex-editorial, political negotiator of loans would be blessed with a success which would be most satisfactory to the southern portion of our country, however it might be to the northern!

Yet such a course, in regard to the slaves, is certainly in accordance with the "precedents" which are by some attempted to be inwoven, in these days, into the law of nations. The "precedent" of Napoleon and the Russian serfs, before alluded to in these pages, has been already sufficiently discussed in the newspapers. It was his first downward step toward the gloomy exile in which he died; and, if our government would but take the same step, the result would surely be gratifying to the southern portion of the country, if not to the northern. Yet Napoleon was not herein a repudiator; so this precedent does not come quite up to the point at which it would be completely "apt."

An apter precedent, one quite in point, is the case of *Jehovah* v. *Pharaoh*, alluded to also some pages back.

If we follow that precedent, we shall surely gratify the southern portion of our country, — I mean, the disloyal whites there, — if not the northern. The "case" is reported at length in the book wherein we read, "Cursed be Canaan." It is as follows:

There was a ruler over a certain country called Egypt, and the ruler's name was Pharaoh. A pestilent fellow, one Moses, troubled Pharaoh with appeals in behalf of a hated set of slaves, whose color did not suit the people of Egypt. It is thought, moreover, that their odor was not good. At length, trouble came; Moses pretended, that the trouble came from God. But be this as it may, it came so thick and hard that Pharaoh was at last induced, as a matter of pure military necessity, in fighting off this trouble, to issue a much-talked-of Emancipation Proclamation. When the proclamation was fully out, and had done its work, the trouble abated. Then said Pharaoh, "I did not go into this war with the trouble for the sake of freeing the slaves; the trouble is over, and the masters consent to keep the slaves,—I should like to see the man who will say, that I will not condescend to make peace by withdrawing the Emancipation Proclamation. The proclamation is withdrawn; the *status quo* is restored."

Well, the godly in all ages are doomed to suffer; so was this godly ruler, Pharaoh. Once more came the trouble, and it came in a form worse than at the former time. I need not extract the whole report, the reader knows where to find it; he has seen it often when searching for those blessed words, "Cursed be Canaan;" let him look at it once more for himself. The end, like the end of all saintship, was sublime. That swim in the Red Sea! who can paint its beauties and its glory? That song of triumph and of thanksgiving which went up on the other side of the sea! who has read it without emotion? Let me turn to the record here: "The Lord is a man of war: the Lord is his name. Pharoah's chariots and his host hath he cast into the sea: his chosen captains also are drowned in the Red Sea. The depths have covered them: they sank into the bottom as a stone."

Leaving the "precedents" here, let us turn back and look again at the Proclamation of President Lincoln.

In estimating the Proclamation, we have to consider two things,—What were the powers of the President?—What did the President attempt?

It is obvious, on a mere outside view without any minute examination of the matter, that the President, as the chief of the nation, was authorized to pledge the nation's faith to the performance of those duties which the Constitution enjoins upon it. We have seen, that one of those duties was to give liberty to the slaves in the seceded States, and incorporate them into the body politic there. And although the Proclamation is not in express terms based on a recognition of this duty, and although it does not promise a complete performance of the duty, yet, on a principle familiar to the legal profession, it is nevertheless good as such promise as far as it goes, and a recognition of the duty may be considered to be implied in the promise.

Plainly such a promise was highly important, not to say necessary, at the time it was made. The very active and vigilant Church of the Cursers of Ham had its priests and its ministers abroad throughout this whole country, and its missionaries abroad in foreign lands, proclaiming everywhere, that the Creed and the Constitution were one, therefore that the Constitution forbade the doing of the thing which we have seen it expressly enjoins. Congress had neglected to perform its part by the enactment of a statute to meet the case, and the inference was strong, and the wicked world without took it to be irresistible, that the church had in league with her herein the whole governmental power of the country. Well, therefore, did the President fulfil his office, when, by proclamation, he dissipated this imposture. The Constitution, Art. II. § 3, provides, that "he shall from time to time give to the Congress information of the state of the Union, and *recommend to their consideration such measures as he shall judge necessary and expedient.*" He had not recommended to Congress the passing of any law in obedience to the duty of clothing the seceded States — that is, the States which had denuded themselves by the act of secession — in those new governmental State garments, which, because of the necessity produced by the rebellion of the whites, must be woven, at least in part, of ebon-colored wool. Neither had Congress taken action upon this subject. Yet both the President and Congress had called up the military power to subdue the rebellion; and to the President it seemed fitting — so we may reason from the act itself — that he should announce to the country, and especially to those not-disloyal persons in the southern part of the country whose services were needed, the governmental determination to obey, in the degree pointed out, the behests of the Constitution.

There are few questions, outside the dominion of mathematical truth, upon which some differences of opinion, varying in degree, are not entertained by different persons. In the previous pages of this pamphlet, and in my pamphlet entitled "Thoughts for the Times," I have expressed my own clear conviction, that it was the duty of Congress to provide, in the beginning of the war, for this new clothing of the revolted States. Nevertheless, the fact stands out in clear relief, that new State governments cannot be practically organized in these States, except as fast and as far as the Union's war-power overcomes the rebel arms. My view of this matter is, that the members of Congress should attend strictly to the duty of making the laws, and the soldiers in the field should attend strictly to the duty of fighting. Neither the soldier nor the congressman — such is my opinion — should rest, while any thing remains to be done belonging to his particular department. If the law for reclothing these denuded States could not be made available in the shape of clothes actually put on, until the stern hands which are wielded by our country's war-arm had taken up the wool, picked it, carded it, spun it, and woven it in our all-glorious freedom-loom, still this is no reason why the vote to have the clothing-work done should be withheld, as though the voters hoped for the opportunity to dodge the vote.

Yet in the actual state of this world, it is not wonderful that the President and Congress should have adopted the course which was pursued. Too few are the men who are content simply to do, and to do promptly, their own duty; and who, when this duty is done, can look up and "read their title clear to mansions in the skies," unappalled by the fear of being pulled down to perdition by the sins of some wicked neighbor. I showed, in my "Thoughts for the Times," that this war would not have been, but for the saintly horror of the South at our loose holding, in the North, of the tenets of the Church of the Cursers; and our unwillingness to be bound by all the new bands which the southern Cursers, more orthodox than the northern, kept continually forging for their heretically-inclined northern brethren. Had the more saintly southern branch been content to go alone with its negroes to heaven, leaving the erring North to its chosen outer darkness, there to be howled over only by unearthly demons, the Nation had not now been drenched in blood. So, had Congress been content simply to perform her duty under the Constitution, not demanding to be let off until the army had first done its part, she would not only have pursued the wiser course, but her members would also have fulfilled the obligation of their several oaths of office. Yet, as man is, it could hardly be expected that the men of whom our national legislature is composed, should have done otherwise than they did.

I look, therefore, upon the President's Proclamation, as embodying — I am not now saying how much more it embodies — the nation's pledge, that she will carry out the requirements of the Constitution substantially in accordance with the interpretation of it given in the foregoing pages. When the Proclamation was completed by the issuing of the part which was dated January 1, 1863, the two houses of Congress were in session; and, though their attention was called to the matter by unhappy members who disapproved of it, no resolution or act of dissent was or could be passed by either House. Therefore, although a negative is not generally, in legislation, equivalent to its opposite affirmative, yet this negative may be deemed to amount to an expression of the opinion of the legislative body, that the President was competent to pledge, in this way, the faith of the nation, and that Congress concurred with him in giving this particular pledge.

There is, as the reader knows, another view of the Proclamation; and, according to this other view, it is an act in the nature of military legislation; done, by competent authority, in the course of legitimate military operations. This other view appears, even more distinctly than the one I have just presented, upon the face of the instrument; but it is not within the scope of this pamphlet to discuss the Proclamation in this other aspect. Yet equally in this other aspect as in the one before mentioned, it is a pledge of the nation's faith.

Some persons there are who profess to regard this Proclamation as a thing of no validity of any sort; and who are not ashamed to say, that they shall rejoice, when, at some future time, three million negroes are rebound in chains which they were told by a white President, a white Congress not contradicting, had been broken; and the *status quo* is restored in the midst of the hissings and hootings of a civilized world. If ever such a carnival of hell is held in this country, may I *not* "be there to see!" Were I a negro, though of an age and physical constitution not adapted to war, still I would enter this war as a soldier, not dreading the previously-announced determination of the southern white power to play the barbarian toward me, by murdering or enslaving me, if captured, in disregard of the most sacred rules of all civilized warfare; I would fight as a good and obedient soldier under my white officers; but if, after I had helped in overcoming the enemy, the United States should make up with the conquered rebels on the condition of reducing me or my kindred or my color to slavery, in violation of the promise contained in this Proclamation of the President — some white lawyer, or judge, or bench of judges, having pronounced it unconstitutional, — I, too, would then play, in turn, the barbarian. Being placed outside the Constitution, I should not regard it as binding upon me. Being denied any rights under it, I should acknowledge to it no allegiance. The North and the South having become alike barbarians as to me, I should make myself a barbarian as to them. While I could cling to life, I would slay by poison, by the hatchet, by any thing, whatever wore a white face! And if innocent babes fell with the guilty aged ones, so let it be! My every exertion should be to slay! to slay! And when at last I fell, I would gather up, in the skies, the souls of my slain; and wear them as gems in a coronet of glory, which I would put upon my head! Blessed angels should hover around me, and sing to me their lays of war and of love. Peaceful music should float to me from the bowers of bliss. God should bless me; and all his universe of happy ones should shout amen! amen! as the smoke of the torment of my persecutors rose up forever and ever.

CHAPTER VI.

CONCLUDING SUMMARY.

The reader perceives, that there are two classes of authority relating to the questions discussed in this pamphlet; namely, the authority of our revered Church of the Cursers of Ham, and the authority of the Constitution of the United States as expounded by our Supreme Court. But for the teachings of the church on this subject, no doubt would be entertained by any person as to what are the teachings of the Constitution. And the reason why I have been compelled to fill a hundred pages with what would be sufficiently plain stated in a single page is, that, whenever the voice of Law speaks, it falls upon ears filled with the roar of the hallelujahs of our church. Could I obtain, but for a single moment, the ear of the most devout worshipper of the church, being likewise the most determined detester of the law, when the ear was swept clean of this hallelujah roar, I could, even in this short space of time, impart to him more wisdom concerning our Constitution than I expect any son of the church to derive from this entire pamphlet.

Let me, therefore, close by setting in contrast the Catechism of the Church, used for infant minds, with a brief Catechism concerning the Constitution:

CATECHISM OF THE CHURCH.

Question. Can you tell me, child, who made the United States?
Answer. Not the great God who made heaven and earth.
Ques. Who, then, made the United States?
Ans. The several States, and the people thereof.
Ques. Who made the Constitution of the United States?
Ans. The several States, and the people thereof.
Ques. Who made slavery in the slave States?
Ans. The great God who made heaven and earth.
Ques. Why did God make slavery in the slave States, yet did not make the United States?
Ans. This is a mystery which he has withheld from the wise and prudent, but has revealed unto babes. Matt. 11 : 25.
Ques. Please explain the mystery?
Ans. God makes all the good and bright things, but leaves all other things to be made by inferior workmen.
Ques. Is this the reason why God did not make the United States, but made slavery in the slave States?
Ans. It is, most reverend sir.
Ques. Is this the reason why God made slavery in the slave States, but did not make the Constitution of the United States?
Ans. It is, most reverend sir.
Ques. When the things which men make, and the things which God made, come into collision, which must give way?
Ans. The things which men make, most reverend sir.
Ques. When slavery and the government of the United States come into collision, which must give way?
Ans. The government of the United States, most reverend sir.
Ques. When slavery and the Constitution of the United States come into collision, which must give way?
Ans. The Constitution of the United States, most reverend sir.
Ques. When the decisions of the Supreme Court of the United States, and the decisions of the priesthood who minister to the Cursers, come into collision, which must give way?
Ans. The decisions of the Supreme Court of the United States, most reverend sir.
Ques. What are the tenets of the Holy Church of the Cursers upon the question of submitting to earthly governments?

Ans. There are no earthly governments over the church, but the church sometimes governs earthly governments.

Ques. What is the rule which the church enjoins upon its members concerning their own personal submission to earthly governments?

Ans. The member of the church is to submit to the earthly government as far as that government is governed by the church.

Ques. What is the rule, when the earthly government is not governed by the church?

Ans. The higher law of the church then prevails, reverend sir.

Ques. What is the rule where the people seem to be attached to the earthly government, yet the earthly government does a thing not previously sanctioned by the church?

Ans. It is to *blacken* the thing, reverend sir.

Ques. Please explain the meaning of this term "blacken?"

Ans. "Blacken," reverend sir, is a word which takes its significance from that blest emblem of the church, a bowed negro clasping a crushed spirit which the church has in training for heaven.

Ques. To what is the term "blacken" or "black" applied?

Ans. It is applied to all negroes, as I have just mentioned.

Ques. To what else is it applied?

Ans. To whatever else the church wishes to *crush*.

Ques. What is the vulgar term which the ungodly sometimes use to signify the same thing as blacken?

Ans. Lie, reverend sir.

Ques. Is it ever right to use this ungodly word, when speaking of the saints?

Ans. Never. It is not only wicked, but it is also highly impolite.

Ques. Name some things which the church blackens?

Ans. The Emancipation Proclamation, put forth by that heretic, Lincoln, is one of the things.

Ques. Name other things?

Ans. The church blackens all persons who do not join her in blackening the Proclamation.

Ques. What does the church teach concerning those who sustain the Proclamation?

Ans. The teachings of the church are always twofold; first, her teachings to the saints; secondly, her teachings to the outside, heretical world.

Ques. What are her teachings to the saints concerning those who sustain the Proclamation?

Ans. She teaches them, that, unless these heretics are destroyed, the church will be put down; and, with the fall of the church, will fall the power of her Confederate government.

Ques. What are her teachings on this subject to the outside world?

Ans. She teaches the outside world, that these heretics are fanatics, who would destroy the Constitution of the United States, pervert the war from its original purpose of suppressing rebellion, and never bring it to a successful conclusion.

Ques. What teaches the church to the outside world concerning the duty of this country in such an emergency as this?

Ans. She teaches to the outside world two things; namely, first, that the church is the only expounder of the Constitution of the United States, and that it is not safe for the common people even to read it; secondly, that the people must stand by the Constitution as the church expounds it, and spend their strength in supporting it, as thus expounded, but give no strength to the government in its struggle to save the Constitution from being rent in twain by the church's blest Confederacy.

Ques. Does the church, when addressing the outside world, speak of her Confederacy in the language which you, babe, have just employed?

Ans. When the church addresses the outside world,— that is, the world of heretics and of sinners,— she uses holy guile in her speech; therefore, in order to save her reputation, so as to secure an influence with those whom she would win, she describes her Confederacy as only a combination of an abused people striving, unwisely perhaps, to defend and protect menaced rights.

Ques. What are the teachings of the church to the saints concerning their duty to the Constitution of the United States?

Ans. She teaches the saints, that it is the first duty to overthrow the Constitution of the United States.

Ques. What is the teaching of the church to the outside world concerning that clause of the Constitution which says: "The United

States shall guarantee to every State in this Union a republican form of government?"

Ans. Her teachings to the outside world, upon this subject, vary with the persons addressed. Here, she would be all things to all men, that she might by all means save some. 1 Cor. 9: 22.

Ques. Give some examples of her teachings on this subject?

Ans. To the very ignorant, she asserts that the Constitution contains no such provision.

Ques. What saith she to such of the outside world as have read the Constitution, and know this provision is in it?

Ans. To some she saith, that it doth not contemplate any such state of affairs as exists in the United States at the present time.

Ques. When these reply, that, this being so, and it not being incumbent on the United States to guarantee to the seceded States republican forms of government, it is best for the United States to govern these States as conquered provinces, or as territories,— what saith the church then to such heretics?

Ans. She doth not condescend to reason with heretics who have become so vile; but she saith to the rest of the outside world, that inasmuch as, plainly, beyond all scope for discussion, the duty of the United States is, not to govern the seceded States as conquered provinces or as territories, but to give them republican forms of government, — a point expressly guaranteed in the Constitution itself, — those heretics who proposed such a gross outrage ought to be roasted over slow fires, then burnt to crisp, and then their ashes given to the saints to be used for snuff, seeing this unholy war hath made tobacco dear.

Ques. Hath the church other methods of dealing with such vile heretics?

Ans. She proposeth, that, when this war is over, all heretics be burned, and thereby peace be secured to the country.

Ques. What saith the church to the class of heretics who would take the church at her own word, and give again to the seceded States republican forms of government?

Ans. She saith, that, by the Constitution, traitors who have undertaken to overthrow the government of the country, their treason having been prompted by their great love for the church, are not for this reason, disqualified to be voters under the Constitution; bu that fanatics, and negroes, and all such creatures, who have not known enough to be disloyal to the government, are, by the Constitution, disqualified: so the United States must give to the seceded States governments based on treason.

Ques. Which, of all the answers made by the church to the heretically-inclined outside world, is deemed to be the most convincing?

Ans. The point of making snuff has hitherto been the most powerful point put by the church.

Ques. Is this point always to be deemed the most powerful?

Ans. The church hath a prophetic vision, that this point is to be superseded by the point put a little way back; namely, that none but traitors know enough to carry on republican forms of government, therefore that they must be selected in the seceded States to carry on such forms.

Ques. If the negroes knew enough to carry on republican forms of government, would there be any objection to permitting them, and loyal white persons, in combination, to carry on such forms to the exclusion of the traitors?

Ans. Seeing the traitors will not carry on such forms, there would be one objection only, which is, that it would be impossible any government could stand, which is not built upon the rock of the church.

Ques. Why could not the government of the United States stand, without resting on the rock of the church?

Ans. There are many reasons, most reverend sir; but the reason which this babe can give is, that the government could not stand without a Constitution, that there can be no constitution without an expounder thereof, and that the church permits none but herself to expound the Constitution of the United States.

Ques. What would be the effect of the church's permitting outside sinners to expound the Constitution of the United States?

Ans. It would be equally disastrous as if she permitted fanatics and heretics to expound it.

Ques. What would be the effect of permitting fanatics and heretics to expound the Constitution of the United States?

Ans. There are no words adequate to convey the idea of the effect; it would be terrible.

Ques. What would be the effect of totally overthrowing the church in this country?

Ans. The effect is one which could not be contemplated; in the first place, the Constitution would be killed; that is, the constitution of the church.

Ques. What amount of knowledge is it necessary, by the Constitution of the United States, as expounded by the church, a voter should possess?

Ans. He need not possess any worldly knowledge; but he ought, properly, to possess that knowledge which consists in understanding the catechism of the church.

Ques. Does the question of freedom or slavery depend upon how much the person who is to be made a freeman or a slave, knows?

Ans. It does not; but here is a point, very nice indeed, not given to babes to explain. It is taught to the saints, that all persons who do not understand the mysteries of the church, and all persons who earn their bread by the sweat of their brows, — brow-sweat being detrimental to true religion, — ought to be made slaves. Here is a mystery which this babe cannot fully explain.

Ques. Suppose the negroes do not know enough to vote, is that a reason why they should not be made free, so as to lend their support, though not as voters, to the republican governments to be established in the seceded States in the place of those which the rebellious people overthrew?

Ans. No, that is not the reason; but the reason is, that the tenets of the church do not permit negro slaves to be made free.

Ques. Is there any provision, corresponding to this blessed tenet of the church which forbids freedom, to be found in the Constitution of the United States?

Ans. The church teaches, that all her tenets are so many distinct parts of the United States Constitution; otherwise, there is in the Constitution no such provision.

Ques. Does not the Constitution guarantee, that, though a State secedes, still slavery shall be permitted to stand in the State?

Ans. This is a provision, reverend sir, clearly laid down in the articles of our holy church.

Ques. Are not the articles of our holy church deemed by all saints to be superior to the articles of the Constitution?

Ans. They are, reverend sir.

Ques. Is it to be tolerated for a moment, that the Constitution should ever be set up above the church?

Ans. Never, for a moment, reverend sir.

Ques. If any man attempts to set up the Constitution above the church, what does the church do?

Ans. Blackens him, most reverend sir.

Ques. What saith the church about such a man?

Ans. She saith that he is a fanatic.

Ques. What else saith the church?

Ans. She saith that he is a radical, reverend sir.

Ques. What else saith the church?

Ans. She saith that he is an enemy to the Constitution, reverend sir.

Ques. What more, saith the church?

Ans. She saith, that, when this war is over, the man is to be *crushed*, reverend sir.

Ques. Is the church always to triumph?

Ans. Prophecy telleth of a beast that is to make war with the saints and to overcome them. Rev. 13: 1, 7.

I perceive that the Catechism is quite too long to be inserted entire in these pages. There are few demagogues who do not know it all by heart; and the specimen here given will serve for those readers who are not instructed in the demagogic trade.

CATECHISM OF THE CONSTITUTION.

Question. Are the seceded States now States within the Union, or are they out of the Union?

First possible Answer. They are out of the Union. [The result of this answer, the reader sees, is, that we should let them go. This is what the rebels claim.]

Second possible Answer. They are in the Union, but they are no longer States. [Then they should be governed as conquered provinces, or as territories. This is a result which all persons among us who call themselves "conservatives," have hitherto scouted, as a political heresy almost as bad as secession itself.]

Third possible Answer. They are yet States in the Union, and they have State governments. [Then their senators and representatives sit in the Capitol at Washington, their State officers are sworn to support the Constitution, and so on. This is what everybody knows is not true in fact, it is not recognized as fact by the authorities at Washington, or by any other authorities or people on earth; therefore this answer is not admissible.]

Fourth possible Answer. The seceded States are still States in the Union, but they are denuded of their State governments. [This is the position of the present pamphlet.]

Question Second. This fourth answer to the first question being assumed to be correct, — Is it the duty of the United States to clothe these denuded States in governments republican in form?

First possible Answer. It is not. Neither Art. IV. § 4, of the Constitution, nor any other clause, applies to the case. [Then the conservative part of the country has been, from the first, in the wrong. There is no limit, therefore, to the power which the United States government has over the seceded States. As there are no governments in these States, the full governmental authority, as known in public law, is in the United States; since the existence of any portion of the country without government is a thing not admissible in theory, and not possible in fact.]

Second possible Answer. It is for the seceded States to clothe themselves, of their own motion, in loyal governments, under the Constitution of the United States. [This is what the particular persons, in the seceded States, who took the States out of the Union, have refused, and still refuse, to do. Other persons in these States are willing. This answer, then, brings us to the doctrine maintained in this pamphlet, namely, that the willing should be permitted — by congressional act authorized — to execute their desire.]

Third possible Answer. The negroes are too ignorant to carry on State governments. [This answer takes us into a field of discussion not lying within the province of this pamphlet. The Constitution of the United States has not declared them to be too ignorant, and the object of this pamphlet is to discover what is the law.

CONCLUDING SUMMARY.

The Supreme Court of the United States holds, that they are not disqualified by reason either of ignorance or of any thing else. As a question of fact, negroes carry on governments in Hayti, in Liberia, and in other places. Whether they are too ignorant or not, is matter of private opinion, not of law. According to the opinion of the dominant classes in the Old World, common white people are too ignorant. Our laws have discarded that opinion, and discarded also the same opinion as applied to negroes. Yet, in fact, should the negroes be permitted to exercise civil rights in the seceded States, the governments would not be negro governments; for the white element would, even then, be the controlling one. There is a much stronger probability, that, under our naturalization laws, the people of some foreign country will become the governors of our native-born people, than that, under the law of our Constitution, enforced in the seceded States, the negroes will become the rulers over the whites.]

Fourth possible Answer. The United States must clothe these States in republican governments under the Constitution; taking for the purpose, the material which presents itself, namely, the negroes, and the loyal whites.

This last answer brings us again to the doctrine which this pamphlet maintains. It is what the writer believes to be the doctrine of the law. *And in all the discussions which the times have brought out, no man has yet appeared to controvert, on any basis of legal authority, this doctrine.* Those who have combated the assumed right of the United States government to give freedom to the slaves in the seceded States, have directed their arguments against other views of the Constitution than those put forth in this pamphlet, not against these views.

Ye ministers of the Church of the Cursers! bring now on your learned lore. Present one authority, recognized in our law, against some one proposition, to be by yourselves selected, out of the many legal propositions laid down in this pamphlet; or else acknowledge, that the doctrines of your church are not the doctrines of the law and the Constitution of this country.

It is not for me to say, what a Curser can find when he turns over the books of our law. I will close this pamphlet with this statement, namely, that it has been my almost constant study, since the mutterings of the coming tempest of war were first heard among us, to ascertain what the law, as actually adjudged by our courts, and held by writers of authority, taught concerning the matters discussed in the pages of this pamphlet, and concerning the other legal questions involved in our present troubles, and that I have not — I now speak particularly of that part of the pamphlet which follows the first chapter — found one line written by any judge, whether on or off the bench, or by any writer of recognized correctness of opinion, contradicting any one proposition stated herein to be law. If another man finds what I have failed to find, let him announce his discovery to the public; but, until he does, *let him beware how he attempts to lie down the truth.*

POSTSCRIPT

ON THE PRESIDENT'S PLAN OF RECONSTRUCTION.

At the time when the foregoing pages were stereotyped, the President had not presented to the country his plan for what is called reconstruction of the seceded States. According to this plan, the power in these States is to be put back substantially into the hands of those persons, who, to rebel, violated their oaths to support the United States government and Constitution, on condition of their taking the oath over again; and those who shall have helped the government of the United States, and shall have remained loyal, and shall have broken no oaths, are to be left to the mercy of the oath-breakers by whom the rebellion has thus far been carried on. Yet the whole country, except such persons as wish the rebels to succeed without the necessity of breaking any more oaths, applaud the plan! It may be politic; of this I cannot judge. It may be a religious duty to build up the powerful wicked, and oppress the feeble good; of this, those in the community who are holier than I, must decide. The readers of the foregoing pages know, that, in these respects, it is a plan violative of the Constitution.

The reader is requested to forget here, that there is any such being as a negro; or, if he prefers, let him deem it conceded, that the negroes have no rights, and that those parts of the Constitution which give them rights are to be held as null, because in conflict with the high duty to curse these children of Ham, both in season and out of season. He will then not object to the President's proposition to offer no rights, except the mere naked one of personal freedom, to be exercised by those men of the South, who, with colored blood in their veins, shall have helped save the country.

Looking, therefore, only at white people, how stands the matter? The persons who are to reconstruct governments in the seceded States are to be those, and those only, who are entitled to vote according to the old State constitutions as they stood at the breaking out of the rebellion. According to these, in some of the States there are property qualifications which serve practically to exclude most of the real friends of the Union, but always to make voters of the rebels. In Louisiana, Arkansas, and Texas, there was a provision in these words: "No soldier, seaman, or mariner in the army or navy of the United States shall be entitled to vote at any election in this State;" whence it follows, that those patriotic white men, who, in these States, have entered the National service and fought the rebellion, are not to be permitted to vote in establishing the new State governments; but every perjured man, from the rebel service, who has done no such disqualifying act as to pledge his life to preserve his country, yet who has pledged it to destroy his country, can vote. In Alabama the provision was, "that no soldier, seaman, or mariner in the *regular* army," &c.; wherefore. in this State, if the patriotic white man judiciously discriminated, and took a particular department of the service, he might retain the privilege of standing on the same high footing with the late rebel soldier.

Still. I bless God that there has been some advance. The President's Message has made known to the country, that there is in the Constitution the provision which I have quoted and principally commented upon in this pamphlet, concerning the guaranteeing of republican governments to the States; and, what is another advance, he proposes to obey, and recommends Congress to obey, this provision by-and-by, though not now. The work of being *politic* is to be attended to first; obedience to the Constitution is promised when this shall have been done, and when oligarchies, composed of one tenth or so of the former voters. who have rebelled, and excluding the mass of the always loyal men, shall be set up to govern the loyal in those States!

Another thing has been gained. It is now conceded that new governments are to take the vacant places which secession left open in the seceded States. If the time shall come, when Congress is disposed to provide for the establishment of these new governments, as the Constitution commands, perhaps the following draft of a bill may be suggestive to the committee to whom the matter shall be referred. It is an expression, in legislative form, of the idea, speaking through the times and circumstances, embodied in the constitutional provision which now commands legislation:

An Act to carry into effect Art. IV., § 4. of the Constitution.

Whereas there are at present no governments of States, recognized by the authorities of the United States, in North Carolina, South Carolina, Georgia, Florida, Alabama, Mississippi, Louisiana, Tennessee, Arkansas, or Texas; and whereas the Constitution of the United States requires the establishment of such governments in those States,—

Be it enacted, &c., That for the purpose of establishing such governments, and unless and until this provision shall be changed by the constitutions to be framed for those States respectively by the people thereof, all male citizens of the age of twenty-one years or more, and all other male persons born in the United States, who shall actually inhabit those States respectively, and who shall be loyal to the Constitution and government of the United States according to such test as the President may establish, shall, irrespective of color or condition, be entitled to vote as electors.

SECT. 2. All persons of African descent, so entitled to vote, and their children and families are hereby declared to be free persons and citizens of the United States.

SECT. 3. Such new governments shall be established in each of said States, at such times, and under such regulations, as, consistent with this act, the President may adopt and direct.

SECT. 4. The constitution of each of said States shall contain a provision securing personal freedom forever to all persons within the said States, except persons charged with crime, or convicted thereof, or imprisoned for debt, and the like; and a provision, likewise, in the nature of a contract with the United States, not to molest any person thereafter, by reason of his having served the government of the United States, or having been or remained loyal thereto, during the present rebellion; and not to reduce to servitude any person made free by any act of Congress, or by any Proclamation of Emancipation issued by the President.

www.ingramcontent.com/pod-product-compliance
Lightning Source LLC
Chambersburg PA
CBHW020142170426
43199CB00010B/851